RETURN TO ADVENTURE SOUTHEAST ASIA

With Amazing Thailand as the Hub

Diving on Wrecks
Jungle Safaris
Spelunking
Taking the Train
Motoring
Bird Watching Expeditions
Trekking the Hill Tribe Country
Searching for Lost Cities
Mountain Climbing
River Exploring
Archaeology Digs
Island Hopping
Biking
and
Other Adventures
in Southeast Asia

Copyright @ 2000 by Harold Stephens
Photographs by the author, except where stated

Printed by Allied Printers, Bangkok, Thailand
Cover Design/Layout: Robert Stedman Pte. Ltd., Singapore

Publisher's Cataloging-in-Publications
(Provided by Quality Books, Inc.)

Stephens, Harold
    Return to adventure Southeast Asia: with
    amazing Thailand as the Hub / by Harold Stephens
    –1st ed.
    p. cm
    "Diving on wrecks, jungle safaris, spelunking,
    taking the train, motoring, bird watching
    expeditions, trekking the hill tribe country,
    searching for lost cities, mountain climbing,
    river exploring, archaeology digs, island hopping,
    dirt biking and other adventures in Southeast Asia."
    LCCN: 99-75810
    ISBN: 09642521-6-3

    1. Asia, Southeastern–Description and travel
    2. Adventure and adventurers–Asia, Southeastern
    3. Stephens, Harold–Journeys–Asia, Southeastern
    4. Title

    DS522.6.S74 2000   915.9'0453
        QB199-901847

Wolfenden
P.O. Box 789
Miranda, CA 95553-0789
Tel: (707) 923-2455 Fax: (707) 923-2455
E-mail: wolfen@northcoast.com
Website: http://wolfen@wolfenden

Also by
Harold Stephens

Discover the Orient
Malaysia
Destination Singapore
Singapore After Dark
Turn South at the Equator
Asian Adventure
Motoring in Southeast Asia
Asian Portraits
At Home in Asia
Three Decades of Asian Travel &
Adventure
The Last Voyage
The Tower & The River
Who Needs a Road?
The River of Kings

Return to Adventure Southeast Asia
is dedicated to
Prajak Jamrusmechoti
of Thai Airways International
who over the years put up with my oftentimes wild
ideas and sponsored many of my adventures.

This book is a collection of true stories and true happenings. The places are real and the incidents took place as the author can best remember them. Some of the material has previously been published in the *Bangkok Post, The Asia Magazine, Living in Thailand, Signature, Travel & Leisure* and Thai Airways International's in-flight magazine *Sawasdee*. Several chapters appeared in the author's previous travel book Asian Adventure, published by MPH in Singapore.

With special thanks to
Thai Airways International
and
Tourism Authority of Thailand Los Angeles
and to
James Erkel and Sandy Holman
for their editorial contribution

RETURN TO ADVENTURE
SOUTHEAST ASIA
With Amazing Thailand as the Hub

Southeast Asia from south China to Indonesia, including Burma in part, Hong Kong, the Philippines and Borneo.

SOUTHEAST ASIA:
MORE THAN GOLDEN TEMPLES AND GOOD SHOPPING

Return to Adventure is not a guide book, nor is it intended to serve as such. Rather, it has been written to introduce readers to a side of Southeast Asia that has long been ignored–Southeast Asia's world of adventure.

That Southeast Asia has an intriguing and alluring outdoors may come as a surprise to many. We have fixed images of Asia that are hard to overcome. The very mention of Asia and our minds conjure up all kinds of preconceived ideas. Take Thailand. Thailand presents an image of enchantment that's hard to dispute. It's a land of golden temples with tiny bells that tinkle in the breeze; a country with green mountains, tropical forests and endless offshore islands; a nation of smiling people and happy children, and monks in saffron robes moving in silent animation; a country interlaced with rivers and canals, with rice barges, teak logs floating down rivers, ferryboats and river buses all gliding along in a kaleidoscope of changing colors.

This image of Thailand is real enough, but it's not the complete picture. Thailand is more than golden temples and smiling faces. Thailand has adventure lurking in its midst, at every turn. Its mountains are a challenge for both rock climbers and mountaineers; its wild rivers churn with white water for daring rafting and kayaking; it has trails to hike or cycle through majestic hilltribe villages and lovely tropical forests; it has ocean floors littered with wrecks to investigate; it has ancient ruins and archaeological sites still to be uncovered; and for the spelunker, amateur or professional, it has caves to explore. The fact that Thailand has unexplored caves is news to some, but even more astounding is that these underground caverns number in the tens of thousands. The caves of Thailand are only one of the country's greatest mysteries.

The image we have of Thailand may be incomplete, but

The image we have of Thailand may be incomplete, but we can't forget the other countries of Southeast Asia—Malaysia, Singapore and Indonesia to the south; and Burma, now Myanmar, to the west; and to the east, all of Indochina, Laos, Cambodia and Vietnam. Nor can we forget the Philippines, and all of East Malaysia that is Sabah and Sarawak on the island of Borneo. They all, even tiny Singapore, have their images, beneath which lie the hidden world of adventure.

It is not foreign travelers alone who are unaware of what Southeast Asia's outdoors has to offer. I know a Chinese family in Singapore, typical Asians, and good friends, who went on vacation to Los Angeles and returned home filled with excitement. What had impressed them the most? Disneyland. They raved about a boat ride they took up a jungle river. They traveled 9,000 miles to see a fake jungle, and yet less than a hundred miles to the north of their home in Singapore they could have seen the real thing, the last great jungle of the world—the Oriental jungle. Imagine, the oldest, untouched rain forest on this planet, a jungle that teems with wild animals and illusive aborigine tribes who make the forest their home, and they settled for Disneyland.

Asia outdoors is hard to sell. Years ago I was invited by the Malaysian chief game warden to join an expedition that was taking stock of the wild elephants. The expedition was successful and got a great deal of press coverage. A Singapore travel company, upon reading about the expedition, came up with the idea of introducing jungle safari trips to foreign tourists. To promote the idea, the travel company asked me to assist in producing a short travel film. It was a fun assignment depicting a weekend safari into the jungle. When the editing was complete, the agent went off to Europe and America with the film tucked under arm. "I'll have clients flocking to the jungles," he said.

A month passed, then another, and another. A half year came and went, and not one person, not one, signed up for a jungle safari. The agent sold shopping and sight-seeing tours, but no jungle tours. It wasn't that people were against jungle bashing and wild animal watching. It's just that they were content to sit in Raffles Hotel in Singapore and listen to the bartender at the Long Bar tell them about the tiger that was shot under the billiard table back in the 1920s. It didn't matter the tiger had escaped from the zoo. And tourists felt comfortable just to sit in a Tudor-style hunting lodge (but no hunting, please) in the Cameron Highlands in Malaysia knowing that outside their very door was a forest where elephants and tigers roamed.

Tastes in travel do change. Travelers are beginnibg to want something different—adventure. For years, it seems, even the spirit of adventure was dead. It wasn't so long ago that whenever I talked about going off to explore the jungles of Borneo or about sailing aboard a trading schooner in the Pacific, people would scoff. "You can't do that anymore," they said. "Those days are gone."

Today it's quite different. People are interested in adventure. It's obvious from the books and magazines we read, from the films and television programs we watch. Adventure is the theme. Newspapers carry tales of adventure; social clubs invite lecturers to give talks on travel and exploration; adventure clubs have become popular; and there are 'adventure tours' that promise to take you to faraway and often hard-to-get-to places, usually for handsome fees. Whatever the motive or reason, the reawakening of adventure is very encouraging. We all share this earth together, and it can be a very exciting place if we let it be. Adventure, or call it discovery if you wish, adds a new dimension to our lives. It gives us purpose.

We often confuse this "reawakening" of adventure with nostalgia, that is, dreaming of a return to the "good old days." Movie films and TV drama depict the past, and we become lost in reverie. And certainly when we read the pages of Somerset Maugham and Joseph Conrad, and the book on our lap falls shut, our imagination runs back through time. "Those were the days," we sigh. "To have lived a hundred years ago!"

Granted, a hundred years ago, or even thirty or forty years ago, the world was very different, but how few of us ever stop to realize that adventure is not something in the past. It's now. It's happening all around us, all the time. The problem is knowing where to look. We turn to new horizons.

Southeast Asia is a new horizon, a vast unknown land. People look askance when I mention this. Despite the fact that the bulk of the world's population lives in this region, there are still areas, mainly the jungles and mountain plateaus, that remain unexplored. Stone Age people continue to be discovered in the Philippines, and there are tribes of Punans in Borneo who have never seen an outsider.

This is today. What about yesterday? We haven't begun to scratch the surface of Southeast Asia's past. Written history began when the first Europeans arrived. But the Chinese and Indians had been trading by land and by sea for as many as 5,000 years. They had well established trade routes, trading posts and even cities, centuries old and long forgotten by the time the Portuguese arrived. Early Chinese chronicles from the Seventh Century AD make mention of such cities, or trading posts, located up the dark rivers of the Malay peninsula. Yet no one has uncovered these sites. It seems that modern man is more interested in finding oil than in discovering another Angkor Wat.

Thai fishermen sparked off the spirit of adventure a few years ago when they located a wrecked Chinese junk in Sattahip Bay in Thailand. It was a sensational discovery. Its cargo contained priceless Sawankaloke pottery. How many hundreds—perhaps thousands—of other such vessels were lost through thousands of years of trade? In the relatively short span of 500 years, England claims to have had 220,000 wrecks along her shores. Think of Asia, where few divers have ever ventured.

A number of years ago I was assigned by the *Straits Times* to write a book on Malaysia. The paper provided me with a researcher to help with background material. She was a bright

Indian girl studying at the university. Halfway through the project, I was invited to join the jungle expedition I mentioned, but not wanting to dismiss the researcher I asked her to find what she could on prewar wrecks. Six weeks later when I returned, she had located more than 200. When I delved deeper into her findings, I learned to my astonishment that she had not only pinpointed many of them, but that no one had even thought to salvage them. When the Sattahip wreck was found later, I checked through my notes and discovered she had documented it. I have written about this in detail in the chapter "Treasures Beneath the Sea."

An incident that has always fascinated me was the sacking of Malacca by the Portuguese in 1511. Malacca was an incredible port, even larger than Genoa and Venice at the height of their glory. The Portuguese commander, d'Albuquerque, spent some nine months loading his ship with the spoils and riches of Asia. Three days out of Malacca bound for Europe, the ship was lost in a squall off the coast of Sumatra. The wreck has never been found, nor, to my knowledge, has anyone ever looked for it.

Marine archaeology and treasure diving are not for everyone. Maybe you would prefer to explore remote places — not jungles but islands. To explore the islands and rivers of Southeast Asia, I built and outfitted my own schooner *Third Sea*, and found that the world Joseph Conrad had described in his novel *Lord Jim* was not dead. Imagine sailing into a port in Java, where Macassar trading schooners tie up to the quay, side by side, forming a line a mile long. These schooners, with jutting bowsprits and ratlines running up the rigging, measure a hundred feet long. They have no engines; they enter port by kedging, just like the square riggers of old did. For the daring adventurer, it's possible to find a berth aboard one of these schooners and sail with them to any one of the thousands of islands that make up the Indonesian Archipelago.

Or imagine sailing in the shadowed sides of islands where smoking volcanoes rise up from the blue sea, or stepping ashore on beaches where the descendants of dragons fifteen feet long still survive. And maybe somewhere in that Indonesian chain of 13,000 islands there is another Bali where no tourist has ever intruded. It is possible.

And what about exploring the Spice Islands of the Sulu Sea by local boat? It was this small cluster of islands in the Indonesian archipelago that sent Asian maritime kingdoms to war and sparked off the age of discovery in the 15th and 16th Centuries, prompting Columbus to cross the Atlantic and Magellan to circumnavigate the globe. The Moluccas produced the spices European aristocrats craved. In time the trade to Europe became so lucrative that a vessel loaded with spices from the Far East could make enough profit from one voyage to pay ten times over the cost of the voyage, including the value of the ship. Yet few people today visit the Moluccas.

When you knock around Southeast Asia long enough, you become fascinated by the mountains, and there are some great challenging peaks, all the way from Japan down the Malay Peninsula to Borneo. To reach the summit of the highest peak in central Malaysia you must first chop through primary jungle. It takes a couple of days just to reach the base of the mountain. To reach the summit of the highest peak in Southeast Asia, Mount Kintabalau, you must climb to 14,500 feet. By Himalayan standards it's not terribly high, but when you begin at sea level, it's quite another thing.

It was in the remote jungles of Malaysia, while on a fishing trip on the Endau River, that I heard orang asli aborigines mention seeing oversized human foot prints up river at the source. The possibility that there might be a Malaysian version of Big Foot intrigued me. I began my research and a year later, after getting sponsorship from an American magazine, I led an expedition into the area. We didn't find the Malay yeti but we did discover on a mountain top a prehistoric life-size stone carving of an elephant.

The orang asli themselves, along with the hill tribes of Bangladesh, Burma, Thailand, Laos and Vietnam, are fascinating to anyone interested in anthropology. The Negritos of the Malay Peninsula and the Punans of Borneo still live in the Stone Age. I have lived for a short time with both, but to research their way of life would take a lifetime. In the chapter "On Safari in the Oriental Jungle" I will introduce you to a Negrito, a jungle man I came to know.

In the days when Somerset Maugham traveled in Southeast Asia and wrote about the things he saw and the people he met, the sport was big game hunting. Hunters thrilled in having their photographs taken with a booted foot propped up on the carcass of an elephant. We can be thankful times have changed. The fun today is to chase wild animals, especially dangerous ones, with a camera. There might be more excitement there than one bargains for. On an assignment in Assam at the Kazaranga Game Reserve, I rode with rangers on elephant-back while they checked the wild elephant herds coming down from Tibet. I felt perfectly safe until a rogue elephant in heat broke through the thicket. The elephants we rode were females! I was too preoccupied with my own safety to think about getting pictures. Another time in the Malay jungles I had my orang asli guide lead me to within twenty feet of three wild elephants so that I could get a good shot with my camera. I had to decline. The click of the shutter would have done us in. In Asia it takes much more courage to hunt with a camera than with a gun.

When you are at a jungle camp, orang asli sit around the camp fire at night and tell tales about man-eating tigers that have carried away members of their tribe. It can send a chill right through you when in the black of night you hear a tiger roar. One's immediate reaction is to stoke the campfire, until you remembered that roaring campfires attract elephants. A tough decision to make.

For the spelunker, or cave explorer, Southeast Asia is prime territory. Geologists tell us that Asia was once connected to Australia by a land bridge. For millennia the land has been eroding, leaving many limestone outcroppings that appear like city skyscrapers. Most are hollowed out and deeply caverned, and it was here that early man found shelter. Niah Caves are the best known. Java Man occupied these caves 35,000 years ago. Also well known are the Batu Caves a few miles north of Kuala Lumpur. Thousands of tourists visit the main cave every year, but few ever venture into any of the other caves that extend deep within the mountain.

I came to Southeast Asia more than thirty years ago looking for adventure. As a beginning writer, I made a contract with the *Bangkok Post* to write twelve articles on the area. Thai Airways International was my sponsor. But I was a little worried. How could I possibly find enough material to fulfill my contract? Twelve articles! Many thousands of newspaper articles and magazine stories later, and more than a dozen books, I feel that I have only begun. There is still so much to see and so much more to do.

Return to Adventure is only an introduction to Southeast Asia's great outdoors. Much of the material presented within these pages is based on my own personal experiences, with the hope that it will encourage others to enjoy Southeast Asia's outdoors as I have. Adventure doesn't necessarily have to be hard-core, fighting rapids or climbing mountains. It can be as simple as taking a train trip, getting behind the steering wheel of a car or Jeep and motoring, or joining a bird-watching group. It's all up to you.

HS
Bangkok
May 2000

Chapter 1

DIGGING INTO SOUTHEAST ASIA'S PAST
The Search for Lost Cities

A farmer tilling his land near the village of Ban Wang Haad in northwest Thailand accidentally discovered the archaeological site of an ancient city that predates the rise of the great Sukhothai Kingdom. About this same time on the other side of the world, in the remote jungle of the Dominican Republic in Central America, archaeologists discovered a long-lost city once inhabited by the people who welcomed Christopher Columbus to the New World.

Two recent discoveries of lost cities within the same year. How can this be? How is it possible that a city can be lost in our modern-day 21th Century? How does it become lost in the first place?

Ever since man learned to build great cities, he also somehow developed the knack of losing them. It may sound impossible but it's a fact. Cities simply disappear. When this happens, if it isn't a farmer plowing up his field that makes a discovery, it's the countless stories, legends and myths that keep our imagination fired up. And they have done so for centuries. The tales of lost cities are endless.

In the Western world it started as far back as *The Book of Genesis* which tells of disasters in which whole cities were swallowed up. Even the Greek philosopher Plato got into the act. In his *Dialogues* he writes about the disappearance of Atlantis, where "there occurred violent earthquakes and floods and in a single night and day the island of Atlantis vanished beneath the sea." The search for Atlantis has never stopped.

Asia, too, has its legends and myths. Early Chinese chronicles tell not only of lost cities but lost kingdoms as well. Only recently have we begun to find that they are not all legend, such as the findings in northern Thailand near the village of Ban Chang and the recent one at Ban Wang Haad. Strange and mysterious as it may sound, lost cities in Asia do exist.

The lure of discovering a lost city has led adventurers, archaeologists, men of science and even tourists to probe the earth, to dive to the bottom of the seas, to scale mountains and to hack through jungles. More often than not, the dream ends in disillusion, even tragedy—but not always. Sometimes we find success. Names like Troy, Pompeii, Machu Picchu and Zimbabwe have become household words in archaeology. But how does a city become 'lost'?

Man for centuries has sunk foundations and built cities on shores of sheltered bays, at mouths of rivers, high on plateaus and deep in jungles. But not always did he give thought to the column of smoke rising from the distant, cone-shaped hill. Nor did he consider that the sea would rise up and deluge the land, or that the lake would swell up and swallow his fine temples within their stone walls. Such acts of nature do happen and, strange as it may seem, man does not learn from past experience. Take Tokyo today, for example. Scientists have predicted without doubt that within eighty years the city will be wholly devastated by shattering earthquakes; yet Tokyo is still being built, expanding, growing, and no one seems bothered by the future consequences.

When Marco Polo returned to Europe after wandering across the face of Asia for seventeen years, he spoke of 'the Land of Beach,' which probably was a misunderstood description of Siam or the Malay Peninsula. One begins to wonder if perhaps the Peruvian legend might be true, that the land of Ophir—from which came the riches of King Solomon—lay somewhere in the East. Long before Marco Polo's day, Greek geographers referred to the Malay Peninsula as the "Golden Peninsula."

In the Land of Beach, Marco Polo claimed, was a city of extraordinary beauty and great wealth. Its temple walls were richly carved and it had great courts. A Chinese traveler who followed in his footsteps corroborated Marco Polo's findings and gave firsthand graphic descriptions of the city, which had very lavish courts indeed, and thousands of concubines within.

2

Other source material comes to us from China. Chinese chronicles dating back to the 7th and 8th Centuries AD make mention of two great kingdoms whose capitals were Tambralinga and Langasuka. There's no doubt that they did once exist, but their sites have been lost for centuries.

However, Europeans weren't drawn to the East by legends, no matter how impressive, but by trade. Trade meant ivory and camphor wood, cinnamon and peacock feathers, peppercorn and cloves, and all the fine porcelain, lacquerware and silk to be found in distant, unknown lands. So valuable did these commodities become in Europe that a small bag of peppercorn might pay for the cost of outfitting a caravan across the Persian land routes to Asia.

Centuries before Europeans built their ships and struck out to find the sea routes for themselves, China had a lucrative sea trade with the Spice Islands of Indonesia, which she carried in her vast merchant fleet to the markets of India. Goods that did reach Europe had passed first through India.

Such trade routes were long established. In many cases the merchants found it more profitable to ship their wares to the Malay Peninsula, and from there transport them overland to where Indian merchant vessels were waiting. The route was not only shorter but vessels did not have to contend with unpredictable winds and raging piracy at the southern tip of the peninsula, where Singapore lies today, and the Strait of Malacca.

The first Europeans to arrive by ship were the Portuguese. They brought with them their cannons and swords. Malacca, on the western Malay coast, fell to them and became a Portuguese stronghold. The port with its fortifications gave them control of the East-West trade routes. But still they did not control, or even know, the source of spice trade, so they set out to find the cities of which Marco Polo and the Chinese chronicles spoke about so glowingly.

From 1583 to 1593 they explored eastern Malaya and all of southern Thailand and Cambodia. They could find no great cities, only ruins—and ruins they were not after. They had arrived 300 years too late.

After the Portuguese expeditions ended, the lost cities and kingdoms of Southeast Asia were once again forgotten. The Age of Discovery was passing. Man came to believe that all lands of the Orient and South Pacific were accounted for. Then, not much more than a hundred years ago, a great archaeological discovery was made. Henri Mouhot, a French naturalist, exploring in remote Cambodia, heard tales of a lost Khmer city in the jungle north of Siem Reap. Was it merely rumor? He persuaded a local missionary to guide him there. They traveled first by dugout and then by foot. Finally, after chopping through dense jungle the last few kilometers, they came to a stone wall completely overgrown. Mouhot was stunned. Could this really be? He followed the wall until he came to an opening, and after cutting his way through tangled vines and thorny creepers he stepped through.

What he saw would have turned Indiana Jones green with envy. Before him was a city forgotten for centuries, almost totally devoured by the jungle. Great arches and lintels were heaved

Angkor Wat in Cambodia, built by the Khmers in the 12th century and abandoned by them in the 15th century, was rediscovered little more than a 100 years ago.

upwards. Roots of banyan trees held in their powerful grips the stone heads of gods and goddesses. Massive walls had been split open not by earthquakes or violent eruptions but by the slow overpowering might of the jungle. And where were the inhabitants? There was not a soul, only the cry of birds and the humming of insects as they probed the eerie ruins.

Because it was so overgrown, neither man could fully fathom the magnitude of the discovery—kilometers of roads, hundreds of temples and walled courtyards and an intricate network of canals, moats and waterways.

The Frenchman's discovery was, of course, the famous ruins of Angkor. Angkor was built by the Khmers between 1181 and 1218 and prospered for 200 years, but in the 15th century King Pona Yat decided to abandon his all-too-splendid capital which was vulnerable to the warlike Siamese tribes.

King Pona Yat and his people left the city and went south to the great lake where Phnom Phen is today. Angkor was soon overrun by the Siamese but they did not remain. In time the jungle reclaimed its own.

For many years, when it was still called Indochina, I made a

The author uncovering stone steps at a sacrificial temple at a forgotten Khmer ruin, Wat Ph, in southern Laos, near the town of Pak Se. Photo by Robin Dannhorn.

yearly pilgrimages to Angkor Wat. These remain some of my most enjoyable memories of Southeast Asia. It was simple then to take a train from Bangkok to the border between Thailand and Cambodia and from there travel by bus to Siem Reap. I would rent a bicycle in town and early each morning, with a basket lunch provided by the hotel, cycle to the ruins. The fact that Angkor Wat was a ruin, and jungle eaten, did not detract from her beauty. If anything, it intensified it. She was magnificent, and perhaps one of the finest cities ever built. It was Angkor Wat that aroused my interests in other ruins, and started me on a search for other lost cities of Asia.

Such Khmer ruins are found not only in Cambodia but also in northern Thailand and in southern Laos. Excavation of a major lost city near Champassak was begun by the French prior to World War II but continuous fighting through the years has halted all progress. Occasionally, heads and carved lintels from these ruins show up in antique shops in Paris. I recall an incident that will verify this.

I was traveling in southern Laos with a friend, when, for reasons unknown to us at the time, we were met in the town of Pakse by a military officer riding in a car driven by a civilian chauffeur. He insisted that we go with him, and he then took us to a palace which belonged to a Laotian prince. The building was still under construction, with only the bare shell of a four-story concrete structure standing. The prince, an Asian Falstaff in his late fifties, greeted us warmly. He sat us down at a large table and then gave instructions to a soldier in uniform standing by. Soon an entourage of servants arrived, marching in single file, and carrying cartons of soft drinks, crates of expensive imported whiskies and wines, and buckets of ice. The prince then announced that we would have lunch. I was flattered by his hospitality, and wished that my French was better so that I could converse more freely. When we had finished our lengthy meal and savored his wines and cognacs, he suddenly stood up and motioned us to follow.

We took a flight of unfinished concrete stairs down to the

courtyard and followed the prince to a garage of sorts. He had an attendant open the large, padlocked doors, and then stepped aside. The room was dark and it took a moment for our eyes to adjust. What appeared before us looked like the basement of an old museum. The storeroom was jam-packed with stone carvings, heads and figures, lintels, friezes, everything imaginable that once decorated a Khmer ruin. The prince smiled and bade us enter. Every item was marked and labeled in white paint. I was completely perplexed. Why was he showing us this treasure room? We soon had the answer. He thought I was someone else. He had mistaken me for an antique buyer, a man who showed up with a briefcase filled with green dollars. My friend and I were quietly ushered away from the palace, without the kind prince even bidding us good-bye. I often wondered what ruin he was tearing apart to finance his palace. The prince has since died and I have no idea what became of his unfinished home. But the French antique dealer, I'm sure, got his Khmer treasures back to France.

Champassak was only one such site in Laos. There were more discoveries, chronicled by French explorers in the 1880s, temples and ruins farther to the south which have never been rediscovered.

If Khmer ruins like those of Anger Wat in Cambodia, Wat Phu in Laos and Pimai in Thailand have been uncovered, why not the kingdoms of Tambralinga and Langasuka? In all probability they did exist, if we believe the Chinese chronicles, but finding the ruins will take more than a river excursion through the jungle by longboat or aboard a flight over the treetops by light plane. It will take some deep, hard probing. The jungles have seen to that!

It is difficult to imagine the sheer might and complete destructive force of a tropical rain forest. Leave a seed unmolested on a pavement overnight and it will start to grow by morning. This minuscule seed, carried by a light breeze and dropped into the crevice or crack in a boulder and left to nurture under a tropical sun, will, in time, split the boulder in two. It can turn palaces and cities into ruins, within the short span of a few decades. On expeditions into the jungle, I had set up camps, and when I returned a year later, I could find no trace of my ever having been there.

Although, in time, the jungle destroys, it can also protect. Lost in its midst, a city or a single building may be devastated, but it goes untouched by man. Some years ago while researching a book I was writing on Malaysia, I read in some obscure volume about a Scotsman named Kellie-Smith who had started building an European-style castle on his estate south of Ipoh. He was a rubber planter, and wealthy. What sort of mad idea was this—a European castle in the Malay jungle? I decided to try to locate the castle, if there was one. I had a rough idea where to look, but the area was no longer a rubber plantation. It had reverted to jungle.

On the afternoon of the second day I saw the topmost parts of ramparts on the opposite bank of a muddy river. I crossed the river by a swinging bridge that I found upstream, and followed an old trail through the jungle to the ruins.

The first sight was disappointing. A gate or guard house

Photographer Joe Shaffer, left, inspects Kelley's Castle in Malaysia. Soon after Stephens discovered the ruin more than 20 years ago, visitors began to arrive, and with them came graffiti, with 'John loves Mary' in half a dozen languages.

of sorts had collapsed into a heap of rubble. I had to push aside vines and cobwebs to pass. It was eerie, like stepping on an unknown grave. Beyond the gateway the castle unfolded before me, an unbelievable sight. A spacious courtyard was flanked by arches with parts of the wall and gateways lifted up from their foundations. Trees with trailing vines and creepers grew wildly in the garden. I had to look hard to see the walls of the castle before me, stretching skyward.

I worked my way to the building. Within the massive stone structure there were passageways, dining halls and salons. One stairway led down into darkened cellars, another to more chambers above. Through windows, some twelve meters above ground, the arms and fingers of the jungle were reaching out, grabbing, taking root with fanlike tentacles, and spreading over the thin fabric of the brick and plaster walls. The castle stood like a minor Angkor Wat, and, like at Angkor Wat, gone too were the people. Who was this Kellie-Smith? What happened to him?

I pieced together the story of Kellie-Smith with the help of an old Tamil rubber tapper who had once worked for the Scotsman. It seems that Kellie-Smith began building his brainchild at the turn of the last century. He brought in craftsmen from India, stonemasons from Italy. But then came World War I and Kellie-Smith returned to Britain. He never returned. The rest is history. Since then, Kelley's Castle, as it is now called, has been placed on the tourist map. The jungle has been chopped down, lawns and flower beds planted and the walls of the castle have been marred with 'Johnny loves Mary' scribbled in half a dozen languages. Kelley's Castle had beauty and mystery when I first rediscovered it; today it looks like an unfinished brick building and nothing more. I often wondered, after finding the castle, what would tropical cities like Singapore and Kuala Lumpur be like if they were abandoned and left to themselves for a hundred years. Buildings rising up a hundred stories above ground would be ensnarled, and enshrined, in the grips of mighty trees, with the beauty of nature and man combined.

Could Tambralinga and Langasuka have been consigned to a similar fate as Kelley's Castle, abandoned to the ravages of the jungle? A British scholar and professor of history, Dr. W. Lineham, went to Malaysia with the government service and decided to find out. He gave credence to the existence of the two cities mentioned in Chinese chronicles and placed their location along the Pahang River in central Malaysia. In a report he wrote, "I enlarge upon the importance of Chini as the starting point of a section of one of the ancient trans-peninsular routes to the west of the Peninsula. It is possible that the lake did not always exist in its present form and that it covers the site of an ancient town. I now write in hope that archaeological investigations will be carried out in the Chini region."

His findings sparked off several investigations. Conclusive evidence that there was a settlement of importance at Lake Chini came with discoveries made by J. N. McHugh in 1960 and 1961. He found pieces of glazed stoneware "in glutinous mud" around the lake. These were of Siamese origin and perhaps came from the Sawankhalok kilns. Other fragments with crude dragon-type designs were of the same origin, and date back to the 14th and 15th centuries. In addition, he found a 16th-century Celadon bowl, Ming blue-and-white export ware and a few pieces of Dutch porcelain.

My interest in the lost kingdom developed when I was exploring the upper reaches of the Endau River in search of a reported prehistoric carving of an elephant on a mountain top. Around our campfire at night, our orang asli guides told tales of a sea monster which guarded an ancient city beneath a lake to the north. I was skeptical but curious. Back in Singapore I began delving into old records, unpublished manuscripts and endless rolls of microfilm. Most interesting to me were Stewart Wavell's accounts of his expedition to Lake Chini, the same lake mentioned by the orang asli who were my guides on the Endau.

According to Wavell, his research into the old Chinese chronicles indicated that the kingdom of Langasuka was situated somewhere up one of the rivers in Malaysia. It was a walled city of great importance. I then checked the aerial maps of the region taken during the Emergency in 1950. One map was of the Lake Chini area. For all practical purposes, I could have been looking at a plan of Angkor Wat. Beneath the surface of the lake were squares, possibly walls or canals, a pattern of Khmer cities. I found another item. It was a report by a government surveyor who, while camped at the lake one night, swore he saw a Loch Ness-type sea monster come from the lake and escape into the reeds on the shore.

Aside from dragons and sea monsters, and a few critics, indications still pointed to the possible existence of a lost city at the bottom of Lake Chini. But then the question arises: why a city at all in the Malay jungle? For what logical reason, for what worthy purpose, would the Chinese, or the Khmers or whoever they were build a city or trading post in such an unlikely place? One reason was the difficulty of transporting goods by sea around what is now Singapore.

The sea lanes at the southern tip of the Malay Peninsula are the most hazardous in the world. Winds are unpredictable, currents are swift and strong; seafarers must pick their way through a maze of islands, around shallows and over innumerable reefs and partly submerged rocks. The Chinese traders had good reason for calling Singapore waters "Dragon Teeth Gate." Only after Raffles laid claim to the island were some of the rocks blasted away to provided safe passage. Still, even today, with lighthouses, marked buoys, up-to-date charts, radar and satellite navigation, ships continue to go up on the reefs around Horsbourgh and Lima Channel. How then did these early seafarers manage? How many of them were lost?

The navigational hazards of getting around Singapore to reach the Indian Ocean was only the first obstacle. Another was pirates. Merchant ships were virtually at the mercy of pirates. They plundered at will, without fear of retribution or reprisal. They hid out in their shallow-draft prows in small coves and bays, and swooped down upon helpless merchant ships that had lost their wind. They could move at incredible speeds, with as many as a hundred sturdy men at their paddles, and they attacked without mercy. Piracy until the turn of the century was an aristocratic profession, practiced by many a Malay prince. They enlisted their crews among the head-hunting Dayaks of Borneo. It was an equitable arrangement between master and crew. The Malays took the booty, the Dayaks the heads.

One solution to the navigation and pirate problems was to avoid the southern route altogether. This meant sailing down the eastern Malay coast to a convenient location where goods could be transshipped overland to the western coast, where Indian merchant ships would pick up the cargo. Trading posts and eventually cities appeared on the Malay Peninsula. Langasuka and Tambralinga were two of them.

I went as far as I could with my homework. The next step was to go to Lake Chini, explore the canal that led to the supposed lost city, search the banks of the lake and the islands in the middle of the lake for possible past settlements, and, if possible, make some preliminary dives into the lake — monster or no monster. I was aware that Stewart Wavell had gone to the lake unprepared. To succeed, an expedition would require divers, geologists, archaeologists and interpreters. After nearly a year of planning, I found my team and set out.

It's possible to reach the lake by four-wheel-drive vehicles but we wanted to retrace as closely as possible the route taken by the early Chinese traders. In the 12th century one Chinese traveler visited Langasuka and wrote about his experience in a detailed journal. He traveled for several days up a jungle river which could only be the Pahang, and came to a huge chain across the river which had to be lowered to enable them to pass. It was apparent the Chinese were prepared to keep uninvited visitors away. They did everything to keep the location of their cities well hidden and secret. Other travelers at the time wrote about being blindfolded when they came up the river. The narrow canal was not only their link to the Pahang but it could well have been their first line of defense, like the moats that guarded the castles of Europe. By locks and gates they could control the water level, and perhaps even flood their own city, if they wished.

With some difficulty, we located the canal on the left bank of the Pahang, and there left our longboats. We inflated two rubber rafts and transferred all our gear, including diving equipment, into them. We then poled our way up the narrow, six-mile-long water course called Sungei Chini, or the Chini River. Sharp rocks and stumps protruded from the bottom and we had to portage our rafts and supplies through these areas. We had to negotiate a number of bends, but for the most part the canal ran a straight course. In places it seemed to be a natural waterway, flooded over from the Pahang; but in others, where the banks were steep, the walls appeared to have been dug by hand.

Finally, just before dusk, we reached the lake. We halted in awe at that first view. The lake was far more vast than we had anticipated. It covers several square kilometers, and with fingers like a giant amoebae, stretches out in every direction. We learned later it reaches a depth of fifteen yards.

The water was murky and from the dark depths branches of trees, long dead and covered with green slime, protruded through the surface, looking like surrealistic paintings in the half light. Mangrove trees with gnarled roots grew in the swamps and marshes around the edge of the lake. Bordering these swamps, in deeper water, were thick forests of *rasau,* a type of spiky reed, higher than a man could reach, and so dense we had difficulty poling our rafts through them. They made our progress painfully slow.

The lake is surrounded by jungle-covered hills and over-looked by Gunong Chini, a hill 2,100 feet high. In the center of the lake are two islands, Pulau Balai and Pulau Berhala, the Islands of the Court and Idol.

As dark was falling we reached the southern edge of the lake and in a wooded area set up camp. As we looked at the lake we saw an eerie fog rise up from the still waters, giving the place a macabre appearance. We would not have been surprised had the monster of Lake Chini risen up from the mist at that very moment.

At early light we were aware that we had visitors, orang asli who lived in a village on the opposite shore of the lake. We were able to converse with them in Malay. They assured us there weren't as many crocodiles in the lake as there had been, and that, in any event, they did not harm people. The orang asli regarded them as *keramat,* or sacred. They also spoke about the dragon of the lake, which they called *naga,* and, like the sacred crocodile, they said it was not to be feared but respected.

In a report for the Malay Historical Society, Mr. McHugh wrote in detail about his interviews with the aborigines regarding the dragon. He was told there are two kinds. One has a head with two bumps on it and the other a smaller head like a fowl's. They leave tracks ten inches in width in the mud along the banks. They live in the same area of the lake where the *batu keramat* or sacred stones are located — the same stones we planned to dive upon.

The thought of diving in the lake, crocodiles swimming about and the long lost cousin of the Loch Ness monster coming up from the deep, was not a happy one, but once we began diving we were more concerned about becoming tangled in tree limbs and debris than encountering living creatures of the deep. Our first project was to probe the bottom of the lake and investigate the sacred stones. Visibility in the murky water was only centimeters. We located the sacred stones, where the orang asli said we would find them, a meter below the surface, but when we approached the stones with underwater flash cameras and equipment the movement of our fins stirred up a fine sediment and this reduced visibility further. Photography was impossible. The stones — we found two — appeared to be monoliths standing upright.

The entire floor of the lake was composed of soft alluvial mud, either washed down from the hills or created by flooding of the Pahang. We probed down six meters through the mud and did not touch solid footing. The mud layer could be twelve or fifteen meters thick. Unless the lake is drained, it will require a drill to be put down through the ooze to determine the lake's past history.

We searched much of the perimeter of the shore without success, but on the islands we did discover laterite bricks and a number of pieces of unglazed pottery with cord markings. There was no question that the islands did have settlements at one time in history. But if there really was a city at the bottom of the lake, what happened to it? There may have been a flood that broke the surrounding dikes, or, like Angkor, the inhabitants of the city might have abandoned it deliberately. When troubles came the defenders opened the floodgates and let the waters come, hoping to return one day, which, of course, they never did. In time its very location was forgotten.

If the ancient inhabitants did deliberately flood their city when invasion threatened, then redraining the lake is feasible. But until then, or until some other system is devised, the jungle of Malaysia will hold on to its secret. It is interesting to note, however, that in late 1997, the Malaysian government announced that it was planning to drain the lake "for the advancement of archeological studies." The economic crunch that Southeast Asia is suffering has temporarily put a halt to the project.

Only a short distance from Chini is Lake Bera, and deeper in the interior at the upper reaches of the Pahang is an unexplored land which is called "The Land of the Waterfalls." Aerial photographs show continuous mist over the jungles in the region. What might the jungles hide at Bera or in the Land of the Waterfalls? And where might be the Land of Beach Marco Polo mentioned?

Some day an explorer will find a wall, and beyond the wall will be a city—and maybe it will be Tambralinga.

The author drinks from a vine in the jungle. Muda, right, an orang asli, guided the author on a number of expeditions until he died unexpectedly.

An orang asli family, seen here on a raft on the Lebir River in the Malaysian jungle, shun civilization, contrary to what the author believed before he began exploring the rain forest with the Malaysian Wild Life Department. The family was caught by surprise as the expedition rounded a bend in the river.

Chapter 2

ON SAFARI IN THE ORIENTAL JUNGLE
Exploring the World's Oldest Rain Forest

Scientists call the tropical rain forests of Southeast Asia the "Oriental Jungles." Without question, they are the largest expanse of jungle on this planet, beginning at the Bay of Bengal in Bangladesh and extending two thousands miles eastward. They spread over all of Southeast Asia and include the forests of Burma, Thailand, Laos, Cambodia, Vietnam and the Malay Peninsula. They reach the Philippines and cover most of the Indonesian islands as far as New Guinea and beyond to the Solomons. Much of the forests of New Guinea, the southern islands of the Philippines and the central plateau of the Malay Peninsula, which includes parts of southern Thailand, are the least spoiled, although encroachment is inevitable and on its way.

The Oriental Jungles of the Malay Peninsula are the oldest in the world, so old they make the tropical rain forests of Africa and South America seem adolescent by comparison. While creeping ice fronts were swelling and shrinking across the northern hemisphere, the jungle here slept through an estimated 100 million years of uninterrupted slumber. And while the far reaching climatic changes were affecting the rest of the globe, animal species on the peninsula were forced into new revolutionary channels. Jungle wildlife was left undisturbed and developed into unique species of its own.

The process of evolution is slow and mysterious. Given enough time, under the right conditions, anything can happen. In the upper foliage of the jungle trees, where branches are densely thick and interlaced, there live bizarre specimens. Frogs and lizards which have grown leathery membranes that pass for wings, fly from tree to tree. Most striking of these is the flying lemur, on earth for about 70 million years; it dwells only in the Oriental Jungles. There are also tree snakes.

Living in matted vegetation 150 feet above ground, these

reptiles developed over the centuries without ever coming down to earth, while their nearest relatives elsewhere in the world are the common burrowing kind that have never climbed above ground.

The Oriental Jungles' profusion of rare wildlife stimulated trade in luxuries which has thrived for more than a millennium. Before the days of Kublai Khan, Chinese merchants journeyed to Borneo in quest of exotic medicines, like bezoar stones, extracted from the stomach of monkeys, or rhinoceros horns, used to make cups which could detect poison. Powdered rhino horn is still an expensive ingredient in the Chinese apothecary, just as bird's nest, fetched from caves in East Malaysia and offshore islands along the Thai coast, is to Chinese chefs.

Clouded leopards, tigers, tapirs, elephants, deer, wild pigs and porcupine still roam the isolated hinterland of the Oriental Jungles. But big game is elusive. Due to the denseness of under-growth, animals, other than monkeys and gibbons, are frequently heard but seldom seen. Years of callous butchery at the hand of profiteering hunters have depleted the ranks of some beasts. The one-horned rhino, which Marco Polo mistook for the mythical unicorn, has all but vanished from Malaysia's jungles and is on the verge of extinction. The Orang Utans, the famous "wild men" of Borneo, have been rounded up and placed in a special sanctuary in Sabah.

Many governments set aside vast tracks of land as game reserves, and strict hunting laws are enforced. Game departments have concluded that instead of shooting wild elephants that tear up plantations, they should be captured and relocated in protected parks. Efforts are made to preserve other species.

Our understanding of the Oriental Jungles, or any jungle for that matter, is often misleading. When I saw the jungle in central Malaysia for the first time, while on a fishing trip on the Endau River, I seriously believed it would be impossible to leave the river and penetrate the matted green wall of vegetation that faced us. Furthermore, none of us thought of doing so anyway, for it had to be the same tangled mass of vegetation in the interior as we saw along the river. It wasn't until subsequent trips, when I befriended Malaysia's chief game warden and was invited to join him and his rangers on their expeditions, that I learned how wrong I had been.

To understand the true meaning of a jungle, we must first debunk the myth most of us have about them. The existence of these tropical forests has been known for hundreds of years, but only a very few people have actually gotten to know them—I mean seriously know them. Men has passed around them and floated through them on rivers. Primitive tribes and civilized peoples live on the edges but only a few know what it is like inside, just as I had been misled my first time on the Endau River.

Most adventurers and explorers, including noted British hunters, were not out to study the rain forests, only to make use of them for their own purposes. The name these people generally applied to the forest was "jungle." Scientists consider the word as meaningless as "dinosaur," adopted by the French to mean any and all large fossil reptiles thought to be extinct.

Our concept of "jungle" was further hampered by literary men like Edgar Rice Burroughs, and to a greater extent, Rudyard Kipling. Kipling's intent was simply to give the tropical rain forest the sound of romance. In his jungles, he placed not only animals and plants he had not seen, but others of which he had only heard, whether or not they were even typical of jungles. Kipling's jungles were a never-never land which was so vividly described that readers took it for the real thing. Burrows was a little more realistic.

The world's ready acceptance of the Kipling concept of a jungle is quite understandable. Until recently virtually no genuinely scientific studies had been made of the interior of these closed canopy tropical forests.

Perhaps the reason jungles have been ignored for so long was that man supposed the inside must be an extension of what they could see from the outside. If you look at a jungle from a river, all you will see is a solid green wall of dense vegetation cascading down to the ground from the tops of trees.

This is only a wall.

Then there is the "law of the jungle," widely held to be nothing more than a ruthless competition for survival, a kill or be killed situation. People think of jungle law when they refer to a particularly bitter fight without pity or scruple.

Such competition does exist, but it is not the only rule by which jungle vegetation must grow. There is an interdependence, a mutual aid, and without it the forest could not exist. The jungle plant fights not for itself alone but for the general welfare.

One of the most admired men of the jungle I know is Mohammed Khan, Chief Game Warden of Malaysia, recently retired. I remember him kneeling down to look at fresh elephant tracks, and saying, "Two adult males and a female." He felt the wet earth, like an artist feels the clay he is about to mold. "There are two young ones," he continued. "The youngest is eight or nine months."

We were in the unexplored northern reaches of Taman Negara in the Malaysian jungle, and we were after elephants, to take stock of their dwindling numbers. The elephants had passed only a few meters ahead of us, and although we had not seen them, Mohammed was delighted.

I had met Mohammed years before when he was the acting chief game warden. His love for elephants was obvious from the start. For several years he had been collecting elephant bones, working out a theory. Huge as elephants are, they are difficult to see in tropical rain forests, even at close range. But, because of their heavy weight and enormous foot size, they do leave clear footprints. From these prints he believed it was not only possible to determine the number of elephants in the herd but also their age and sex. Some monsters he measured had feet 22 inches wide.

Over the years, elephants had to be killed in defense of crops and property. Whenever possible the dead animals were measured from head to foot, then quartered and weighed. Their lower jaw bones were removed and a study made of the molars.

Gradually, with enough data gathered over a long period of time, Mohammed was able to see a close correlation between an elephant's foot size, height and body length, and its age.

Not long after that first meeting, Mohammed was appointed chief game warden. He moved to headquarters in Kuala Lumpur, and for the next few years I began exploring the jungles in earnest with the game department.

When Mohammed was still assistant warden he had invited me on my first real expedition with the game department. It was a wild adventure that took us through the green heart of the Malay jungle. We traveled as far as we could by longboat and then began hacking through the jungle. The days turned into a week, the week into a month. On a good day we could cover perhaps six miles. It seemed like twenty. When we followed game trails we moved faster, but more often we had to hack every inch of our way through the jungle. Then as we feared might happen, the monsoons started early. At first, the rains were refreshing. They kept us cool. But when tropical showers turned into down-pours, in the time-worn jungle, things began to happen. We were in a column descending a slope when a loud crashing sound brought us to a halt. It sounded like the roar of an avalanche. A hundred yards ahead a gigantic tree perhaps ten feet in diameter and 200 feet high, splintered in midair, as if it had been struck by high explosives. The unbelievable might of nature—the sheer weight of the rain upon the overhead foliage—had such destructive force that huge trees begun to collapse around us. The trunks would splinter, and then, bullet-like, they would come shooting earthwards, pulling with them other trees, interwoven with vines and climbers. They caused terrific explosions sending debris and showers of rain and mist in every direction. Soon the whole forest seemed to be disintegrating, and we were caught in the middle. We dropped packs and equipment and began running.

But where to? There were no openings. Then ahead we saw light, sky, a river. We reached the safety of the Lebir

River. When the rains stopped, we returned to retrieve our gear.

Two years after that expedition, Mohammed invited me and National Geographic photographer Mike Yamashita to his office. He greeted us warmly, and then pulled back heavy drapes on a wall behind his desk, revealing a huge map of the central Malay jungles. He ran his fingers along the contour of a twisting river. "Here," he said, pointing at a river junction, "right here. This is the place, but unexplored." He turned to face us. "We made careful studies. This may be the last hold-out in Asia for the twin-horned Sumatra rhino."

The search for the rare rhino! It was only thirty years ago that the number of Java rhinoceros was believed to have been reduced to a mere handful. They seem doomed to suffer the same fate as the sperm whale. As late as 1880, when rhinos were plentiful, the Rajah of Perak was paying $50 for horns, which he sold to the Chinese for $500.

With Asian rhino becoming increasingly rare as years pass, a rhino on the black market will bring well over $50,000. So valuable have they become that the Chinese no longer grind up just the horn but the entire carcass as well.

Unfortunately, the rhino's popularity has taken a heavy toll upon the species. According to one estimate, there are but a hundred animals left in Sumatra, and half that number in Malaysia. Thailand has between six and fifteen.

Mohammed was forming an expedition to check the validity of his studies. He then asked what I hoped he would. Did we want to join the expedition? He didn't have to ask twice.

I would like to point out, one doesn't have to know a game warden or be a university professor with a grant to explore the Oriental Jungles. Such expeditions, safaris if you wish, are possible. The question is are they worth the effort? For this reason, let me tell you about the expedition Mike and I made with Mohammed, and then you can decide.

Ten days later after we agreed to join the expedition, we met Mohammed at the river landing at Kuala Tembling for our journey up river to the game department's jungle head-quarters. At dusk we reached our destination and met the rest of the party.

I find any evening before a new adventure tense. There is always some anxiety, and some doubt. That evening was no exception. After dinner we sat with several rangers, talking about the jungle. What is the best way of sleeping in the forest during the monsoon rains? A tiger mauled a Malay boy a short time before. A herd of wild elephants was recently reported in the area we had to pass through.

Outside our verandah the thunder of the monsoons echoed through the night, and occasionally the skies would light up with flashes of lightning. Wild elephants, tigers, raging rivers—even these didn't seem as bad as the prospect of spending the coming weeks sleeping in the wet on bare ground.

Our plan was to travel light, in two long dugouts with two rangers and Muda, a Negrito guide. With eight in our party, we would journey two days more up the Tembling to the Sepia and travel the river to the mouth of the Raj—some 120 miles distant. Here we would make our base camp from which we would strike out to explore the surrounding terrain on foot. There were several high mountain ridges, and an aerial relief map showed a lake of sorts.

Our diet was to be rice flavored with curry, dried vegetables, sugar, coffee and tea. For protein we would depend on the fish we caught in the rivers.

The first morning was far from the rugged expedition we had expected. It was luxury sitting back comfortably, as though we were out to enjoy "the jungle trip" at Disneyland. The river was high and there was no need to get out and push the boats in the shallows. We sat back and watched the jungle pass by.

Our long, slender boats bent and swayed with the rhythm of the river. The helmsmen, who controlled powerful forty-horsepower outboards, took their signals from lookouts on the bows. These men stood with long poles to ward off debris floating downstream, or rocks that might suddenly appear.

We zigzagged from bank to bank to catch the deeper currents. The jungle loomed heavily on both sides, with its thick wall of greenery reaching to the banks. Here, certainly, is man's last refuge on earth.

Thoughts are interrupted by the sight of white water ahead. Rapids. From a distance they appear menacing. Lookouts take position, poles prepared. Helmsmen, instead of slowing down, give full throttle. Boats leap ahead and with full force strike solid walls of churning water. Somehow we always manage to splash through, unharmed. We lose count of the rapids.

The afternoon sun comes out hot, turning the forest into a furnace. In two days our faces and arms are baked brown like dark mahogany.

The further up river we traveled, the more signs of wildlife we saw. With a trained eye the game warden pointed to the jungle. A patch of bamboo was crushed: "Elephants have been feeding," he said. An object that looked like a log on the bank: "Monitor lizard," he noted. Two shadows leapt into the current: "Otters," he explained.

Mohammed was the first to see wild dogs drinking in the river. A great winged bird rose from the rocks, flew into a dead tree overhead and watched us pass. "Osprey," he told us. And when we stopped to eat, he explained the sounds from across the river were "white-handed gibbons" while those on our side were "siamang." After a few days we could tell the difference ourselves.

While the afternoons were hot, the nights were usually cold and wet, sometimes with the full fury of thunder and lightning crashing and lighting up the jungle night. Nature in the jungle is intimate. You are akin to everything about you. Sometimes you don't run for shelter when it rains — you stand looking up at the skies. And on dark nights, it's with God-fearing curiosity you view the jungle world.

We reached the Sepia and began the grueling task of pushing the boats up river. At an abandoned ranger outpost, we decided to leave one boat. The river was becoming too shallow and the boats could not hold our combined weight. We had to walk along the banks. The other boat, pushed up river by the rangers, was used to transport our gear. Mike and I helped the rangers push the boat when we reached the more difficult rapids.

We came to one six-mile stretch of rapids. It took the labor of each one of us to get the boat through, sometimes inching it along. The thunder of water became so loud and threatening we had to shout to be heard. Beneath the surface, rocks and boulders were slippery, and even with careful steps we would suddenly be swept off our feet. Survival meant holding on to the boat, even when completely submerged. Minutes after being drenched in the rapids, our clothes would dry under a scorching sun.

In the open stretches between the rapids it was always peaceful. The jungle appeared in all its pristine beauty. Trees reached towering heights, while some were bent far over the river, with trailing vines and folds of moss and wild plants.

In the soft sand along the banks we found game tracks. We followed those of a wild pig, perhaps only two or three hours old, only to find father up river a tiger had come out of the forest and taken up the pursuit. The tiger prints were the size of a man's open hand.

Everywhere there were signs of elephant. The thought of them charging through camp at night was frightening. When we first set up camp, Mike and I had the urge to light a large fire to keep the elephants away.

"Elephants are attracted to fire," the warden explained.

"Then let's not have a fire," Mike and I said.

"Fine," the warden replied, "except for one thing. Tigers don't like fires. You have your choice. Elephants or tigers."

After that, one night we might have a roaring fire, the next night only a few hot coals. It usually depended on what tracks we saw last before darkness, elephants or tigers.

If you let your imagination run wild, fear of the jungle can be awesome. One evening, for example, after camp was set up, I went down river to fish. In the sand along the bank I had noticed tiger tracks, but gave them no serious thought. I rounded a bend, and with my back to the jungle, cast a line into the still water. It was that hour before dark when all the jungle grows still. No bite. I cast again, and the only sound was the swish of the line. The first fingers of darkness were beginning to close in. Across the river the shadowed side of the forest turned dark purple. Somewhere in the distance a lone monkey gave out with a shrill cry and gave me a start. Then I remembered the tiger tracks. I was soon spending more time looking over my shoulder than concentrating on my fishing. I imagined a tiger coming out of the forest, taking half a dozen leaps, and me fighting him off with my fishing rod. I lost no time getting back to camp.

Once inside camp everything is set right. An evening meal around the fire, hot coffee, pleasant conversation. Soon everyone drifts off to their lean-tos. You retire and tuck your mosquito net around your ground cloth. You lie back listening to the sounds of the jungle in the night. It's incredible, but that thin curtain-like netting is the security that separates you from the hostile world outside.

The journey was having its effects. Traveling on the river was exhausting. We all limped, and it took longer to recover during rest breaks. If it wasn't the blistering sun, it was the relentless rain. Setting up camp and lighting a fire each evening took hours. Furthermore our supplies were running short.

It was a happy moment when we reached the mouth of the Raj. We had traveled deeper into the Malay jungle than any outsider before us. Our success now depended on Muda leading us safely through the jungle.

At dawn the next morning, we cut through the jungle wall east of the river and began our trek. It's astonishing how, once you cut through this seemingly impenetrable wall, the forest changes. On the floor of the jungle where the sun penetrates only in pencil-thin shafts of light, the vegetation is less dense. Game trails are everywhere. If it weren't for the trailing vines and thorny lianas that tear at your clothing, trekking would be easy, certainly much easier than traveling on the river.

Once we had cut trough the wall, Muda, with all the skills of a jungle man, led the way, swinging his razor-sharp knife, clearing a path for us to follow. Now and then he stopped, turning over branches and leaves to check for signs of rhinos.

Aside from thorny creepers we were plagued by leeches. Against all the precautions we took, they miraculously managed to get inside our clothing—except for Muda who went half naked and could whisk off a leech when it first took hold. Within minutes these small creatures, feasting on blood, can swell from the size of a matchstick to that of a golf ball. One does not feel the bite—the only agony is that the wound caused by the leech does not stop bleeding for hours afterwards.

A day's hike from the Sepia, high on one of the ridge tops, Muda suddenly stopped. He motioned for the warden. He had found the first sign. It was not more than a broken sapling. "Rhino," the warden said, elated.

My education in tracking rhinos began at that moment. These great gallant beasts, I learned, dine solely on the leaves of certain jungle trees. By using their horns they snap off the saplings about one meter from the ground. As we penetrated deeper and deeper into the black forest the signs became more frequent. We had reached their feeding grounds. Broken saplings were everywhere.

We realized before we began the expedition that our chances of actually seeing a rhino in the wild were almost nil. It is indeed rare for anyone to stumble onto one. They are caught by poachers who set up snares leading to their wallows, and are left to die a slow and agonizing death.

But here, where man had not set foot before, it was quite different. We were on a trail that gradually widened, and in the distance we heard a sucking sound, as though someone was caught in a mud hole with rubber boots. We rushed forward in time to see a magnificent twin-horned rhino leave the wallow and climb a ridge. And about us, other rhinos fled.

We had found their home grounds. The warden and Muda were able to deduce the number of animals in the area from the tracks and trails around us.

We spent several days exploring the range. The beauty of walking through primeval land was overpowering. We could almost feel plants around us growing; new life, new forms taking shape, the all powerful jungle, nature in its wildest, most wonderful form, untouched by destructive mankind. Every step brought some new and wondrous discovery. Elephants and tigers came to the streams to drink side by side, giant carp swam towards us rather than away from us. So clean and pure was the water we could drink directly from the river.

To cover more ground, we split into two groups. Mike and I went with Muda. Our object was to see if we could find more signs of rhino. We stopped and sat on a fallen tree to rest. An Argus pheasant somewhere ahead called to its mate and a band of gibbons echoed in the treetops close by. All about us was the unending hum of insects. Then came a sound we hadn't heard before, a kind of growl. It was low-keyed. A few minutes later we heard it again, but closer. A third time! Whatever it was, it was moving around us. We looked at Muda. He muttered softly a word we had heard often before: "Limu." We knew the meaning—tiger.

We also knew immediately, without asking, our next course of action. We began our sudden retreat, the shortest way possible, directly down the mountain side to the river. Our arrival at a steep cliff high above the river didn't slow us down. Our arms and legs were still swinging, in mid air, when we landed in the river.

Rains had raised the level of the river. What had taken endless days coming up stream, we were able to do in a fraction of the time on our return. Never would we enjoy soft beds and white sheets more than we did the night we reached headquarters. Muda returned to the jungle.

Chapter 3

TREASURES BENEATH THE SEA
Scuba Diving for Pleasure and for Profit

The development of scuba diving equipment in 1944 by Jacques-Yves Cousteau was destined to have its effects on Southeast Asia in the decades that followed. It opened up a world of adventure no one ever thought possible before.

In the beginning years, scuba diving, an acronym for Self-Contained Under Water Breathing Apparatus, was a commercial business, and as a business, it was controlled by a select group of professional divers. Gradually, however, with new and better scuba equipment available on the market, at affordable prices, recreational diving became possible for thousands of nonprofessional divers. Scuba diving was soon the fastest growing sport around the world, and with it came the search for new diving locations. The warm waters of the Mediterranean was the first pleasure divers' Mecca, and from there it spread to the Caribbean, the Florida Keys, the islands of the South Pacific, and finally Southeast Asia. But it wasn't until this last decade that Southeast Asia's underwater world really became world known. Commercial diving was not new to the area; it had been going on ever since the rich oil deposits were discovered off shore in the 1950s; but it was pretty much a closed door to outsiders. Then came the pleasure divers looking for new locations. Thailand, the Philippines, Malaysia, Indonesia, they all soon became their targets, and for reasons that were not kept secret. Thailand alone has 1,633 miles of coastline with beautiful beaches and countless offshore islands. The Philippines has more than 7,000 islands in the sun, and Indonesia another 13,000 islands stretching across a thousand miles of tropical archipelago.

The advantage of diving in the warm waters of Southeast Asia is that it's possible to enjoy scuba diving all year round. The best time to dive on the east coasts of Thailand and Malaysia is between June and October, when the Southeast monsoon is blowing, and between November and April or May along the west coasts during the Northwest monsoon. The Philippines are to be avoided in the late summer and fall during the typhoon season.

While diving for pleasure is the quest for many, there are others who might be interested in marine archaeology, and for this, Southeast Asia is wide open, an undiscovered field. In the Mediterranean, it all started in the search for Greek and Roman amphora-laden galleys, which eventually led to the quest for sunken gold-laden Spanish vessels in the Caribbean.

While advances in marine archaeology and discovery are constantly being made in the West, such work in Southeast Asia until this last decade was virtually unknown. A significant hint of what lay beneath the Asian seas came when sunken Chinese junks were found by Thai fishermen off the Sattahip coast in the late 1970s.

On hundreds of previous occasions Thai fishermen had found bits of pottery in their nets but had not thought much of it. But in late August or early September 1974 when five fishermen brought home three unbroken pieces found in the course of untangling their nets in the sea they were informed by a knowledgeable person that the pieces were "priceless" antiques. In bounding good spirits, no doubt, the fishermen returned to the place of their discovery and managed by diving to collect 82 more ceramics. They reportedly sold the lot to a Bangkok businessman for the equivalent of $1,200.

The secret location of the fishermen's treasure ship was revealed, however, when a diver, following a subsequent trip, was hospitalized with the bends, a result of rising from a deep dive too quickly without decompressing. The story appeared in the *Bangkok Post*, and before long the sea lane some twelve nautical miles southwest off Khram island in the Gulf of Siam was swarming with Thai fishermen aboard their trawlers, and local and foreign sports divers aboard chartered boats. The resort town of Pattaya found itself enjoying prosperity as business increased. In a six-month period, a half dozen dive shops opened. Fishing boat skippers found it more profitable hooking scuba divers than fish.

The Sattahip incident highlighted the fact that the Asian undersea world was virtually unexplored. Yet the history of the region is filled with accounts of sea voyages, voyages that had often resulted in countless wrecks that had scattered their remains on the ocean floor.

China had sent her junk fleets on expeditions of trade and exploration to far reaches of Asia for some 2000 years. Long before the first Portuguese arrived on the Asian scene, one Chinese admiral, Cheng Ho, reached Malacca with a flotilla of 62 vessels and 37,000 men. His gift to the sultan was a daughter of the Emperor of China, who was given in marriage, along with a fine dowry of 500 handmaidens to serve her.

Admiral Cheng Ho's epic voyages–he made seven in all–were among the very few which have been documented in Chinese chronicles. We do know for certain from these records that cities in the region of Southeast Asia were actively engaged in overseas commerce at a time when Rome was only a minor trading post. Ships of a dozen eastern nations plied the Asian seas for centuries, and how many spilled their treasures on uncharted coasts or submerged coral reefs can only be a matter for conjecture. The future for marine archaeology in Southeast Asia is limitless.

What lies beneath the shallow seas of Southeast Asia is anyone's speculation. Scuba divers tell tales of finding the bones of wrecked Chinese junks that contain Ming pottery. In 1810, a Dutch ship with a cargo of Ch'ing export ware had a skirmish with pirates off Pulau Aur on the eastern coast of Malaysia and was driven into shallow water where she eventually broke up. Pieces of pottery still wash up on the shore after a monsoon storm.

In one of the villages three large iron cannons of European design are on display. One cannon is inscribed with the date 1782. They are believed to come from a Portuguese wreck, but as to which wreck and where it may be, no one knows. More recently, during World War II, a Dutch submarine was sunk in 150 feet of water in the shadow of Pulau Aur.

Malaysia's seas hold untold riches from ships wrecked by storms or plundered by pirates for the better part of two thousand years. Rumors circulate of hidden treasures buried in caves along the coast and on islands off the east coast of the peninsula. But what isn't rumor is the ship wreck of Admiral d'Albuquerque of Portugal.

For centuries the port of Malacca had been a rendezvous for every seafaring nation. Indians, Javanese, Chinese, Arabs, Siamese—they all sought out the harbor in search of profit through trade, piracy or plunder. And each group in turn left something of its own culture behind to be forged and blended into one of the richest ports the world had ever seen.

Then came the Portuguese under the command of d'Albuquerque. He sailed his fleet up the river and lay siege to the town. The sultan fled and Malacca was sacked.

Three months later, with a fleet laden with the spoils of war, d'Albuquerque set sail, only to watch his flagship the

Malacca during the 18th century. First came the Portuguese, then the Dutch, and finally the British. For hundreds of years, Malacca was an important trading center.

32

Flor de la Mar run aground during the night off the coast of Sumatra and break up in the storm that followed. Survivors were picked up the next morning, still clinging to the wreck. The ship's cargo was never recovered, nor are there records to show that anyone has ever attempted to search for the lost ship. The wreck of the *Flor de la Mar* was one of the first major European shipwrecks in Asian waters.

In much the same manner, Sir Stamford Raffles, the founder of Singapore, sent to England a cargo of historical riches aboard a British merchantman. The ship ran aground, caught fire off the coast of Sumatra and was never recovered.

There's a certain amount of mystery attached to any ship lost at sea, and when there's treasure aboard, anything can happen. Unwillingly, I became involved in a mystery that reads more like a Conrad novel than a true story. But, I assure you, it was real.

I was preparing to launch my newly built schooner *Third Sea* in Singapore, when I had a note from an English lady I hardly knew. She was an art dealer of sorts and wanted me to come to dinner. She said it was a private affair that could be important to me.

I was rather rushed at the time and considered declining the invitation, but then the urgency of her tone was too intriguing to let pass. Unless I accepted the invitation I would probably never find out.

She lived in a posh flat on Holland Road. I was greeted by a Malay servant, and although I arrived later than the time stated on the note, I was the first guest. An elegant candlelit table had places set for four. Soft music played in the background; there was a bewitching mood about the place. My hostess asked me to sit on the sofa while the Malay brought drinks.

"You are going to meet two men," she said. "What they have to tell may startle you, but I promise they are legitimate."

Presently the two men arrived. They immediately went to the bar and helped themselves; apparently they were not newcomers to the flat. We were introduced. They had British accents, Welsh to be exact, which I found difficult to understand. I felt that I was missing half the conversation.

The men were out of place in the surroundings. Their manners were gruff and they spoke harshly. The older of the two, a man perhaps in his mid-forties, was heavily tattooed on both arms. The other man had several teeth missing. When we sat down to dinner I had the feeling I had seen them before.

The suspense was too much. Before the first course was served, I asked directly: "What is the reason we are here?"

The man with the tattoos, without faltering, answered by asking me a question. "How would you like to make a million dollars?" he said.

He had to be crazy. Some get-rich-quick scheme, I thought. No doubt they had a story in mind. Quite often when I meet people and they hear that I am a writer, they will say: "I have a great story for you. I'll tell you what, you write it and we'll split down the middle. We'll both get rich."

My three dinner partners sensed my skepticism. The English lady spoke up: "They have been out to the shipyard and they've seen your schooner."

I knew now where I had seen them. More than once I had noticed them lurking in the background, watching the operation, but had not given them a second thought. Lots of people hung around when I was building my schooner.

"You have just the boat we need," they interjected, and in the next half hour revealed the most unlikely story I had ever heard. It seems the two men had located a sunken World War II submarine off the west coast of Malaysia, near Penang. They were careful not to give me the exact location, thinking, no doubt, the information might be useful to me. The submarine, they explained, was German and had a cargo of mercury, some sixteen to eighteen tons, worth millions on the open market. They had already brought up two tons but when they took it into Penang the authorities had confiscated it.

What they now wanted to do was make a clandestine dive on the wreck, using my schooner. They explained their plan.

The fact that I had not yet placed ballast in *Third Sea,* some ten tons, would make it easy. Instead of permanent ballast I would carry removable ballast, which we would discard at the dive site and replace with mercury. We would even jettison the salvage equipment used to raise the cargo, and then sail for Turkey. There would only be three of us, the two divers and me.

"What do we do with the cargo?" I asked.

"We have all that worked out," they explained. "We scuttle the schooner on a deserted beach, salvage the mercury and we're all set pretty for life."

I declined the offer, and remained skeptical until two months later when I read about the men in the *Straits Times*. They were in the headlines. Indeed, they had found a sunken German submarine, and it did have a rich treasure of mercury. The men succeeded in salvaging another six tons of mercury, but their operation suddenly came to a halt. Three governments, Malaysia, German and Japan, all were laying claim to the wreck and its cargo. That was years ago, and still the claim has not been settled. The divers, I understand, did not receive a cent for their efforts.

The biggest difficulty with marine archaeology, or treasure diving, if you like, is finding sunken vessels in the first place. Even after they have been reported lost in a given area the problem is not solved. Survivors from a shipwreck are less than accurate in fixing positions. Even more confusing is the fact that most vessels go down on the windward side of reefs, where their bottoms are torn out by the coral. Considering that coral can grow a centimeter a year, only a few years are needed for a ship, with its cannon, anchor and cargo, to lose its distinctive shape and outline. And wooden hulls, within a few years, unless protected by sand or mud, will be eaten away by worms.

But even more destructive is the sea itself. Chemical action between salt water and iron objects eventually converts such things as cannon balls into virtually pure hematite. Wrought iron merely disintegrates. Silver, unless protected, becomes silver sulfide. Copper or brass becomes encrusted with a patina. Pottery or earthenware becomes overgrown with oyster shells.

Only three metals, pewter, lead and gold, are virtually immune to destruction by seawater or time.

War wrecks have always been the object of keen salvage operators, and both the South Pacific and Southeast Asia have untold wrecks beneath their seas. I was fortunate to be able to spend a dozen years aboard *Third Sea* sailing the South Pacific, touching upon many islands that were battle sites during World War II. We came upon airstrips with bombers and fighters still on the runways; harbors with hundreds of sunken ships, some in water so shallow we could see them below the surface; caves filled with rusting arms, helmets and mess gear; heavy brass cannons hidden in lonely mountain outposts; and still other islands where the military simply walked off when it was all over and left everything behind.

Over the years, the lagoon at Truk Island in the Carolines has attracted many divers. It was here that the Japanese Navy was finally bottled up and sunk. A place I think is even more spectacular is Rabaul on New Britain, an island off the northern coast of New Guinea. Rabaul was one of the most important targets in the Pacific War. The Japanese captured the port two

Fifty years after World War II, a Japanese submarine is still being used to carry fuel in the harbor of Rabaul. The Japanese held the island throughout the war by digging in. They dug more than 300 miles of caves.

days after they bombed Pearl Harbor. They immediately began constructing one of the toughest, most formidable bastions ever built. It was virtually impregnable. The combined allied forces were unable to recapture Rabaul despite dropping more than 20,000 tons of bombs on the place.

The Japanese at Rabaul surrendered to the Allies only after the war ended. The Australians and Americans came ashore and to their astonishment found 90,000 Japanese, civilians and military, living in an amazing subterranean world. In connecting underground caverns were 382 miles of caves into which ships and even submarines were pulled when air attacks threatened them. The Japanese could have held out for years, and they were prepared to do so.

I spent many exciting days exploring some of these caves. No one has attempted to cover them up or conceal them. They are ignored by the locals. Each cave I explored offered something different. Some had steel helmets by the thousand; others had piles of rusting mess gear and canteens; a few contained smashed medical supplies; one had crates of engine parts; in others there were locker boxes full of files, ledgers, records and books —

Photographer Robert Stedman inspects the wreck of a World War II US bomber, one of the many that he and the author found in the jungle on New Britain island in the Western Pacific.

all eaten through by white ants.

Some allied bombers had, however, been successful. Records show that more than 400 wrecks lie at the bottom of the bay, including an American submarine. Only a handful of these wrecks have been explored by divers.

We met several weekend divers when we sailed into Rabaul Harbor. One Australian engineer and his sixteen-year-old son had been working the harbor for three years. He told me, off the record, that he had earned enough money to retire for life, bringing up brass shell casings and selling them to the Chinese. He was an avid underwater photographer and showed me hundreds of photos of sunken vessels, including a Japanese Zero in shallow water and virtually intact.

Not far south of Rabaul begin the Solomon Islands, where the heaviest fighting of the Pacific war took place. As I have mentioned, entire airfields were lost and forgotten, and in some bays entire navies went to the bottom.

But divers don't have to look to World War II wrecks for excitement. There was hardly an island or an atoll that we visited where there wasn't at least one Korean or Taiwanese fishing boat piled up on the reef. Some of the larger islands had two or three wrecks. On islands that are inhabited, the natives clean out the cargo, leaving the ships with valuable equipment to rust and slowly be broken up by the pounding sea. A salvage boat could make a fortune searching out these wrecks in the Pacific. The natives and the island governments care nothing about the wrecks.

In Southeast Asia, there is a whole new field of undersea exploration. The discovery by diver Mike Hatcher of a Dutch ship that sank in 1724 only a few miles off Mersing on the east coast of Malaysia made history in autumn 1984 when he and his divers brought up elephant tusks and tin ingots worth millions. To preserve what is left, the National Museum in Kuala Lumpur has declared the wreck a national monument. A short time after this, Mike had found the famous Nanking wreck, a find that Christie's in London auctioned off for a reported $16 million.

Some World War II wrecks have been declared war graves and are off-limits. Although diving upon them may be possible, with government permission, nothing can be removed from these vessels. Two such wrecks laying on the bottom of the South China Sea forty miles off the Malaysian coast are the British battleships HMS *Repulse* and HMS *Prince of Wales,* both sunk by Japanese dive bombers during the opening days of World War II.

For several years I had my sights on finding *Repulse*. She was reported to be at a depth 180 feet below the surface, with the bodies of more than 500 British sailors still trapped inside. *Prince of Wales* was in deeper water and would be more difficult to reach.

On a clear December morning, on exactly the same date the vessels went down, I was aboard the 80-foot schooner *So Fong* when we located *Repulse*. There were eight of us aboard, the others all professional divers. It was a joyous moment for all of us, to have found the vessel, but it was an eerie, foreboding experience that followed.

The first view of *Repulse* is over-powering. At 30 feet

A diver reaches the hull of the HMS Repulse at 180 feet below the surface.The British battleship was sunk by Japanese dive bombers during the opening days of World War II. Divers bring up shell casings. Stephens is at the right.

the faint outline unfolds. At 60 feet she begins to take shape and form. You can make out details. But now as you drop lower the hull begins to take over, to dominate the ocean floor. It's impossible to see the ship in its entirety. You concentrate on one feature at a time, maybe a torpedo hole. Everything you've heard or read before about *Repulse* may not have seemed real, until now. All the horror of how that mighty ship sank into this dreadful grave suddenly registers. You can almost hear a pounding from inside the hull, until you realize it's your own pulse beat gone wild.

Each diver returned to the deck of So *Fong* with his own impressions. One marveled at the torpedo holes that had ripped through the old battleship's tough sides. Another was impressed by the four huge propellers that projected from the stern. "You can still see her rudder jammed hard to port," he observed. Most commented on the trailing fishing lines and nets that had been lost by Malay fishermen over the years, and how these added to the eeriness and the overall effect. They told of schools of fish, often in such numbers that they blocked out the light; of the large barracuda, manta rays and the occasional shark, cautious, wary. The entire floor of the ocean was littered with shell casings. One diver reported finding airplane engines still in their crates amidships. A few divers commented on the strange crackling sound that they picked up near the bottom. And there was even laughter when a diver told how he poked his head into a torpedo hole and saw a twelve-foot shark basking inside. "The problem was I couldn't turn around fast enough," he joked.

After the third day of diving on *Repulse*, the last diver to come up unhooked our mooring line from the bottom and we drifted downwind from the wreck. As we sailed back to Singapore, we couldn't help wonder how many more thousands upon thousands of wrecks still remain to be discovered beneath the seas of Southeast Asia.

Diving for pleasure, whether it be among lovely coral reefs or upon shipwrecks, or the search for sunken treasure, it's all there beneath the seas of Southeast Asia.

Chapter 4

SPELUNKING VS SPELEOLOGY
Cave Exploring in Southeast Asia

I was having a drink with friends in the Coliseum Cafe in Kuala Lumpur, one of the few old expat watering holes still left in Asia, when an Englishman down the bar interrupted us. We were talking about cave exploring.

"Why do you call it spelunking? " he asked.

"I beg your pardon?" I said.

"Spelunking," he repeated. "Why do you call it spelunking when you really mean speleology? I am a speleologist, and I'd say I've been interested in the sport some thirty years."

Spelunker or speleologist—it depends on whether you are American or British, or on which dictionary you use. Webster's defines a spelunker as one who explores or studies caves. The word is not listed in the Oxford English dictionary, but speleology is, and it means cave exploring.

The sport of cave exploring is little known in Southeast Asia. There's only one club that I know in all the ASEAN countries that's devoted to it. Yet, beyond any doubt, the caves and underground caverns of Southeast Asia are the most challenging and interesting in the world. And believe me, they are everywhere from South China down through Thailand and the Malay Peninsula and scattered across Indonesia and the islands of the Philippines.

Still, one might ask, what's the attraction of caves?

Unlike the reason George Mallory gave for climbing Mount Everest, "because it's there," cave exploring has another dimension. Caves are not only there, and in great abundance, but they hold many of mankind's most baffling secrets. Caves bear man's earliest records.

In the mid 1950s, in a deep cave in Sarawak on the island of Borneo, an explorer found a grave with human remains. When they were later radio carbon-dated they proved to be more than 40,000 years old, the oldest *Homo sapiens* found to date.

Those remains probably represent man's beginning in Southeast Asia. But it wasn't until about 10,000 years ago that things really began to happen, when early man began to migrate southward and took shelter in the caves of Laos, Thailand and the Malay Peninsula. He left behind his history in burial grounds, on cave walls and in artifacts and implements he abandoned.

Not only do caves concern the past, but there's the living present. Deep in both the Malay and Philippine jungle live small dark people who continue to dwell in the Stone Age. Their sanctuaries are limestone caves.

My own interest in the caves of Southeast Asia began when I ventured to a small town in central Malaysia called Gua Musang, a few miles north of Kuala Lipis. The history department of the University of Malaya was conducting excavations following a report that the local Chinese were destroying the limestone caves at the edge of town. It appears they were after bat droppings, which make an excellent fertilizer. The student departent lost interest when it was estimated that the hardened guano was 500 feet thick and would take years to remove. I heard that the villagers are still fertilizing their vegetable gardens with cave droppings, and science has time to wait.

Anyone who travels by road or train through southern Thailand and down the Malay Peninsula can't help noticing the strange looking outcroppings that rise up sheer from table-flat rice fields. They appear like huge fortresses, or castles. Some may be several square miles in size, and others no larger than a city block. The formations, geologists tell us, are calcareous limestone rock in which a surprising number of sea fossils are found. The rocks are 400 million years old.

The fossils show that the rocks were formed originally in the shallow waters of the warm sea. In time these rocks were uplifted by volcanic thrusts and formed mountain ranges.

The caves themselves are the result of erosion caused by rainwater and small streams and rivers. For millennia the land has been washing down on to the lowlands and eventually out to sea. Some geologists believe that the Malay Peninsula and Borneo were once part of a rugged land mass running the entire length of the Indonesian archipelago, possibly to the Australian continent. It was no upheaval that broke up the land mass but the relentless work of nature, the slow process of wearing down the earth by sun, rain, wind and more rain. Even to this day many parts of the vast South China Sea are unnavigable by larger ocean-going vessels due to the shallowness of the water. Several miles from the coastline the ocean floor may be less than fifteen meters below the surface.

These caves offered natural protection to early man, hunters and food gatherers who sought shelter in caves. They knew how to make fire, and cooked their food with the aid of crude instruments hewn from stones. They called themselves orang asli, or original man.

The early migrations are generally not what we think them to have been. Man did not get up one morning and announce to the clan that they were moving on. It was hardly a conscious effort. A family or a group of families settled in a cave, children were born; they grew, mated, and in time needed more space for their family, so they shifted to the next cave down the line. Twenty generations and the migration has moved a hundred miles.

Also, contrary to what many believe, being a hunter and food gatherer, man did not spend all his time living in caves. He moved in the area around his cave and went there not only for shelter and protection but also to bury his dead, perform religious and mystical ceremonies and decorate these sanctuaries as holy places. Caves such as those at Gua Musang, which are preserved under 500 feet of guano, are time capsules waiting to be opened one day to reveal our past.

The most famous of these limestone caves in Malaysia are the Batu Caves, eleven kilometers north of Kuala Lumpur. Famous as they may be, with several hundred thousand visitors every year, they still hold unsolved mysteries.

Batu Caves were discovered a little more than a hundred years ago when American naturalist William Hornby and Police Commissioner Harry Syers of Kuala Lumpur stumbled upon them quite by accident. Hornby was looking for new specimens for his tropical collection, and Syers, an avid hunter and jungle explorer, agreed to show him the area. They were wandering on horseback when they suddenly and unexpectedly came to a cliff that rose up like a wall before them. They sniffed. The air was heavily laden with the pungent odor of bat droppings.

Bats mean caves, and caves mean all kinds of possibilities. Spurred on the by the stench, the team started climbing. Inch by inch they worked their way up the sheer face of the cliff. Half way to the top they reached a ledge, and there they found the entrance to the caves. Never had they, nor anyone else, seen caves so enormous. They returned to Kuala Lumpur with the news of their discovery. Not long after the discovery, Harry Syers was killed not far from Batu caves when a ferocious saladang, an animal similar to the Cape buffalo, came out of the bush and charged at him with full fury. Syers knelt down, took careful aim and pulled the trigger. The gun misfired. He was killed instantly.

Other expeditions followed in the steps of Hornby and Syers, and before long the local Hindu populace started an annual pilgrimage to the caves to celebrate the festival of Thaipusam. As a gesture of repentance for past sins, devotees carry *kavadis*—wooden frames decorated with flowers and fruit, supported by long thin spikes driven into their naked flesh—to the cave. Others drive long metal bars, thick as a man's thumb and shaped like a spear, through their cheeks. Remarkable, but there is never any blood, nor wounds afterwards. Worshippers must climb 272 concrete steps to reach their holy shrine in the cave. More than a hundred thousand people attend the ceremony each year.

Although the broken mass of limestone at the Batu Caves forms less than two square kilometers, it contains no fewer than twenty caves, some of relatively easy access. Those most often visited are along the southern face. The caves have names such as Hermit's Hotel, Priest's Hole and Fairy Grotto. How they earned their names is anyone's guess, but Cathedral Cave needs no explanation. Under a huge vault pierced by stalactites spreads an empty hollow that is as large as the interior of Notre Dame in Paris. Slanted shafts of light streak down from gaping holes in the ceiling creating a mystical effect. Nearby are the illuminated Dark Caves, with paths leading deep within the bowels of the earth. Some of these can be reached by a lift. A couple of hundred feet from the lower elevator station, one of the relatively small caves has been made into an attractive museum with half-size plaster figures of the Hindu deities.

For the serious-minded speleologist, here is adventure untapped. Only a well equipped party can explore the lower caves properly and safely. Anything may be discovered. Endless rumors haunt the caves. The truth in many cases may never be known. Some sources tell how passages lead from the mouth of Batu Caves to the sea more than 35 miles distant. There's always a tale or two about Chinese Communist insurgents who used the caves during the Emergency. It may be true, for caches of guns and ammunition have been found. We know for certain that the Japanese during their occupation turned the caves into an underground stronghold and ammunition depot. To this day, not all the caves have been explored.

I heard about one speleologist who was exploring one of the avenues in the lower caverns when his head lamp came upon a strange object along one wall. He approached cautiously, and to his horror discovered a human skeleton. By all indications, a party had become lost, and not being able to find their way to the surface, perished in what must have been an agonizing death. What is even more strange is that there is no record of an expedition having entered the cave and becoming lost. The bones of another body, that of a

Chinese man, were found on a ledge, with a note requesting that those who find his body ship the remains back to his birthplace in China. The bones are still there.

Tales of hermits living in caves always arouse interest. The cliffs below the Rochardo Lighthouse in Port Dickson, Malaysia have been home to a Hindu hermit for twenty years. I've climbed down the cliffs several times and have never seen him, but local residents swear he really does exist.

I did meet a real hermit, an old Malay man who lives in a cave on a small island south of Pulau Tinggi along Malaysia's east coast. Tinggi itself is a volcanic island, isolated, with less than a thousand people living in scattered villages along the coast. I was leaving Tinggi late one afternoon, returning to Singapore aboard my schooner *Third Sea,* when I saw this lovely little island to the south. It appeared to have a safe anchorage on the north shore. We decided to spend the night and dropped anchor in five fathoms. We rowed ashore and found the old man living alone in a cave.

At first I thought he was perhaps a fisherman spending the night on the island, but he told us that he lived there all

The author, left, scratches in dust a map of the interior of the cave as a spekunker friend looks on. The cave on the right is on a island in the Andaman Sea. The entrance can only be reached by sea, making it even more difficult to explore.

alone. Unlike most hermits, he was sociable and willing to talk about himself. "Why did you decide to live alone on a small island?" I asked him. He explained in a few words that modern society was too much for him; he didn't like the way it was heading. "And where did you live?" I asked. I was certain he would say Kuala Lumpur, or maybe even Singapore, that these two capital cities were too crowded for him. No, he came from the island of Tinggi, six kilometers away. Tinggi was becoming too modern for him!

Another hermit whose existence I can vouch for is a Thai Buddhist monk who lives in a cave on the Malaysian east coast. He is, in fact, one of the most incredible mystics I have ever met. I met him many years ago and, from what I have heard recently, he is still there.

It was chance that led me to the cave the first time. I was looking for the mountain road to an underground tin mine, reputed to be the deepest in the world, when I became completely lost and ended up in an old rubber plantation. I stopped and asked a tapper where the road led. It was not the road to the mine, he explained. I was on the road to Panching

The entrance to a cave is always dramatic, both alluring and frightening. Many caves in Southeast Asia go unexplored to this day; some, like Batu Cave in Malaysia, have passageways that may lead 35 miles underground.

Caves, where the Buddhist hermit monk lived. The hermit sounded much more interesting than a tin mine. I continued on the same road.

The track led through a dusty rubber plantation. A forest of rubber trees closed around us. The plantation was very old, with tired trees covered with canker and mold. Suddenly the road came to an end. A limestone cliff rose up before me, without warning. It seemed to have materialized from nowhere. When I stepped from the car and looked upwards, the mountain seemed to have no top, but part way up the side of the cliff there was a ledge with a railing. A monk in his saffron robe heard me coming. He was leaning over the railing, pointing to a rickety stairway.

I never expected to find what I did.

It took a bit of awkward climbing to reach the ledge. The monk, an elderly gentleman, introduced himself—Than Acham Sakatapunya. He offered me tea and bid me to be seated. He told me how he had come to the Pahang jungle many years before. He had on a shelf behind him a small shrine with the image of Buddha. He mentioned he was pleased that I had come. After an hour I thanked him and began to leave. He gave me a startled look. Didn't I want to see the cave?

"The cave! Yes, of course, the cave," I said, trying to sound interested. I was anxious to leave, as I had lingered longer than I had planned, but politeness dictated that I please the monk and see the cave first.

We climbed a second set of stairs, even more precarious than the first, and came to a large cave entrance. With the monk leading the way I felt as though I was entering a spook show with Oriental overtones. The path led downwards. It was slippery. Walking was difficult. It took a while for my eyes to adjust to the darkness. Suddenly the monk stopped and pointed upwards. Unbelievable. It was not a cave but a cathedral. Thin shafts of light filtered down through cracks hundreds of feet above. In the half light distances were deceptive. Water dripped somewhere in the darkness. Bats fluttered away.

A young Malay boy who was assisting the monk lighted several grass torches and bid that I follow him into a second cave. It was far bigger than the first. And there, suddenly looming up before us was a giant statue of a reclining Buddha. It had to be more than 30 feet long.

Here was the life's work of a lone Thai monk. How many years of unending labor, carrying sacks of cement and sand and building material up the face of the cliff, how many years did it take to construct this noble monument? It was an achievement, certainly, by both man and god.

I didn't leave that day, nor the next. In fact, I spent the next few days on the mountain top, exploring with the help of the Malay boy. Fortunately, I had camping gear in my car. And when we weren't exploring, we sat with the monk, listening to his tales. He told how he first scaled the cliffs and saw the deep caverns within the mountain. He petitioned the Sultan of Pahang and was granted permission to build a Buddhist shrine in the mountain.

Aside from the two large caves at Panching, there were dozens of smaller caves, and endless passageways. Sometimes we inched our way through halls so narrow I had to exhale to enable myself to pass. We often found ourselves not looking up but down, through cracks into the pits of the mountain.

Even more frightening than the dark, unknown passages were the openings which suddenly led to the exposed face of an outside cliff. Here we had to tie in with ropes and lower ourselves down to other openings. More than once I wondered if we would ever find our way off the mountain.

On one of these high ledges, many hundreds of feet above the green jungle floor, we spent the night. We watched the sun set over distant hills, and later watched the moon rise. We spread out our blankets and built a warming fire. The scene before us, seen from this same ledge, remains unchanged since man first began walking upon the earth. For that one splendid night we were living a part of our vast heritage, and we had a sense of belonging. I now knew why the Thai monk decided to build his shrine at Panching Caves.

The ambitious speleologist, or spelunker, can find more interesting caves along the eastern coast of the Malay Peninsula. While sailing my schooner up and down the coast, I studied hundreds of caves with my binoculars. One set of caves in particular caught my fancy, and later when I was driving up the coast I decided to visit them. The villagers called them "pirate caves."

They are located three kilometers before Kemasik at Milestone 56. A dirt track turns off towards the sea and leads to a nearby sandy cove, backed by a ridge of rocks extending far out to sea. You must climb the rocks to reach the caves. Once you drop over the other side you come face-to-face with the deep chasms.

The scenery is so appropriate to our image of what a pirate cave must look like, you expected to find a treasure chest and skull and crossbones inside. The floor is sandy and slopes upwards. Bats flutter away and it takes courage to enter.

As you cautiously proceed into the inner darkness you find there is a maze of smaller caves and passageways. One leads to the left and exits on a small sandy cove. In a great semicircle, cliffs drop down to the beach. The sea here is blue and clear among the rocks. White birds circle above. All is peace and quiet. But no treasure chests.

Some very exciting caves are found on the island of Tioman 35 miles off the Malaysian coast. Tioman's impressive peaks have been used as a landmark by traders ever since man took to the sea in small boats. The island also has a ready supply of fresh water, and as a result it became a stopover point. The caves served as excellent storage cells and Chinese merchants filled them with their precious wares, many of which were kept in earthen crocks and vases. In time some of the caves were forgotten. The department of anthropology at the National Museum in Kuala Lumpur has opened a few caves and found hordes of priceless Ming pottery and other valuable artifacts.

A few years ago an Australian adventurer turned up on Tioman with a secret map that supposedly led to hidden caves high in the mountains on the southern side of the island. He insisted the caves were treasure-packed, but to reach them he needed a guide. He went to a nearby village and did his utmost to convince the Malays to guide him up the mountain, but, of course, they refused. Caves are taboo to Malays. The man wouldn't give up and struck out alone, against everyone's advice. Five days later he returned, his eyes wide, his voice barely audible, mumbling that he had found them, he had found the cave. Minutes later he died, probably from exposure and exhaustion, although the Malays attribute his death to something else. Nevertheless, whatever the cause, his secret went with him. Dato Shahrum, the Director of the National Museum in Kuala Lumpur, informed me that the caves are still there, somewhere.

Ipoh, an industrial town on Malaysia's west coast, is noted for its limestone caves. Both north and south of the city motorists will notice sheer limestone outcrops. At their base are what appear to be odd-looking buildings, constructed flat against the cliffs. Most of them are painted white with red tiled pagoda roofs. They are in fact only the facades of caves converted into temples, both Chinese and Hindu.

One of the largest of these is Perak Tong four miles south of Ipoh. It contains a number of altars and a statue of Lord Buddha that stands thirteen meters high. Beyond these altars and almost hidden are the entrances to more caves, where the real adventure begins. By following one marked path you can reach an opening 60 feet above ground. There's nothing particularly daring about the climb but it does offer an insight to possible cave exploring in the area.

Some of the most challenging caves I know are found in Thailand, and at no place in Southeast Asia is there such an abundance of caves in such widely dispersed locations as Udon Thani province in the northeast and Koh Khian in Phang-nga and Tham Sin in the south, not to forget all the offshore islands.

Among the countless caves in Thailand, only a fraction have been fully explored. New caves are being discovered almost every day. As I write these lines, a cover story in the *Bangkok Post* reports that a new cave in Ban Nainang Khao Kram had been discovered following a survey trip by Krabi regional tourist officers, Laddawan Chuaychat and Pisut Phumphamorn.

The cave, they claim, is about seventy yards wide and twenty yards high at its gateway. Inside the cave is a 25-yard long beach with a canal that runs through the cave. The officers believe it may be possible to take a long-tail boat through the cave to the other side of the hill.

Most caves in Thailand have guides standing by ready to take visitors on cave tours. They offer not only their service but equipment as well, including carbide lamps. Many Thai caves are listed on tourism maps, but even the best map will not have all the caves marked. Nor does it mean that if caves are marked on tourist maps, they will be overrun with tourists. On the contrary, I've come upon some that hadn't been visited in months, perhaps years. The paths leading to them were

Some caves may be many miles deep. Most caves are carved out of limestone outcroppings and may not be necessarily underground. Early man took shelter in caves and has left his marks on cave walls. Many caves go unexplored.

overgrown and difficult to find. Other were impossible to find. To add to the confusion some caves may have several names.

As we have seen in Malaysia, caves in Thailand aren't necessarily all underground caverns. Many exciting caves are found up high in the limestone outcroppings, hundreds of feet above ground.

A number of remarkable Thai caves can be found along Route 4 in the south which runs through Phang-nga to the small seaport of Krabi. The more popular cave near Phang-Nga is Tham Russi—Hermit Cave. A stalagmite in the shape of a hermit marks the entrance. Many believe the *russi* has power to cure the sick and predict winning lottery numbers. Unusual labyrinthine grottoes weave through the cave where visitors can stroll over bridges crossing pools within the cave. It's well lighted with neon lightd and it even has toilet facilities.

Continuing 500 yards down the road, past the governor's office on the left, a sign points out a trail towards Wat Tham Pong Chang, which translates to "Temple-Cave in the Elephant's Stomach." A claustrophobic tunnel to the left of a pool leads into a small shrine adorned with statues of three sacred elephants.

Since man first entered caves, he has left his mark, whether it be religious shrines or places to bury the dead. Buddhist temples with magnificent statues are found deep within caves throughout Thailand. Monks live in some caves.

Farther south on Route 4 is a splendid cave called Wat Suwannakuha. At the entrance packs of monkeys wait to be fed by visitors, and a sign reads: DO NOT TAKE PHOTO-GRAPHS WHEN YOU ARE NOT PROPERLY DRESSED.

It's one of the few caves that has an entrance fee, but ten baht is worth it. Wat Suwannakuha has hundreds of Buddha's images, including three large golden figures, a reclining Buddha and two large standing Buddhas. A second set of stairs leads to an upper cave with more images. The cave has mood and provides an ideal setting for the photographer.

A mile after Phang-nga, Route 4 reaches a fork where a sign points to Krabi. Beyond the fork the road rises into a winding pass through giant limestone hills and fertile valleys. At the foot of the pass there's a humble view of a Buddha statue at Wat Kirirong, at the entrance to a hollow under huge cliffs.

South of Wat Kirirong the countryside becomes even more dramatic, especially if you are making the drive at dusk. The horizon on all fronts is outlined with the jagged ridges of endless outcroppings, like contorted dragons of another age.

One of the most interesting caves I found in the south was not far from Krabi. It isn't marked on maps nor is it mentioned in guide books. I saw the simple sign that said THAM PETCH, with an arrow pointing down a side road, and decided to gamble. After driving three miles down a dusty road, I arrived at a hut with a rusted tin roof where an old man with a flashlight stood waiting, as though he was expecting me. I parked and he then led me through a dusky rubber plantation over a path not too well trodden to the entrance of a cave. A statue of Buddha stood at the entrance. Nothing too dramatic. I took a few photos and was about to leave when the man bid me to follow him. He lead me to another entrance, and to another adventure.

I spent two days at that cave, and in that time I explored only a few hundred meters, yet the old man claimed the cave was more than seven kilometers deep. At least that was the furthermost anyone had ever gone. The formations were different than other caves I explored. Some chambers appeared to be man-made, with beautifully formed tubs and basins that served as catchments for water, or perhaps they were altars for some strange gods. I wondered if we might discover dens where prehistoric dinosaurs still dwelled.

Another interesting area for caves is in southeast Thailand along Route 3 that leads to the Cambodian border. At the 288-km stone (180 miles), a turn north along a small town street leads to a rough dirt road, and ten miles beyond is Khao Wongse with its jagged outcrops filled with caverns. Some locals who have lived in the village all their lives claim they have not seen all the caves. In the crevices in the face of one cliff, Buddhist monks have fashioned living quarters where they recite scripture.

Northeast Thailand has more than its share of caves. To reach them follow the Friendship Highway, or Route 2. Twelve miles after the town of Saraburi turn on a dirt road to Phra Ngam Cave, or Beautiful Image Cave, which holds a Davaravati-era image. There are hundreds of other caves nearby, most of them unexplored and unknown. Even the villages we talked to are unsure of what is there.

What many consider the most interesting cave in Thailand is Tham Pha Thai along Route 1 between Lampang and Ngao. Sixteen miles before Ngao, a left turn leads to a small grove of teak trees, with an information board and map and a nearby refreshment stand. To reach the cave entrance requires a climb up 283 concrete steps, some broken by roots, past the monks' quarters, to the huge arched entrance to the grotto. In front of the entrance stands a white *chedi* while immediately inside beneath the sunlit edge sits a gilded Buddha. Behind the Buddha rises a colossal stalagmite from a sea of limestone.

The cave is noted for its slithering green snakes which wrap themselves around electric wires or coil up in crevices. The snakes are protected and it's said they never have bitten anyone. The first 400 yards are open to the public. The walk ends at a mound of bat guano where a thin column of light streaks down from a jagged opening in the cave roof, projecting the silhouettes of flying bats onto the cavern walls.

The area around Chiang Mai in the north has some spectacular caves. The best known is the Chiang Dao, 42 miles north of town. I reached the cave just before dark and found the lights had been turned off, but for a hundred baht the attendant found me a guide, and with a hissing gas lantern he lead me into its depths. We came upon chamber after chamber, with Buddha images crammed everywhere. With only our gas lantern lighting our way, shadows leaped out at us and sent chills down my back. Nagas guarded the passageways and in the dim light they became alive and seemed to follow us as we passed, making grotesque silhouettes.

Traveling north to Fang, past the Hmong village Ban Hua Toa, a turnoff leads to Tubtao Caves. At the end of the track steps lead to Light Cave on the right and Dark Cave on the left. The caves are steeped in Buddhist lore and are said to have been created by the cremation fire of an early devotee.

Doi Inthanon National Park west of Chiang Mai is a major tourist attraction, with a very interesting site—Borichinda cave. A further two-hour drive from Chiang Mai leads to Mae Hong Son, one of the more remote towns in Thailand. Worth a visit are the nearby Tham Pla, or Fish Cave, the larger Tham Lod cave.

Nor should we forget the River Kwai area. The 60-room River Kwai Village makes a good base for travel and organizes trips to nearby caves. One trip is by boat. On the way to Sai Yok, the river passes the Cave of Tham Kung with some every impressive stalactites and stalagmites.

These are the known caves. What about lost caves, and how can a cave become lost? Landslides, violent storms, earthquakes, volcanic upheavals, and by man himself. It's a known fact caves for some reason or other are sealed by those who want to keep them secret, as the Japanese did to many caves in Southeast Asia after their defeat in World War II.

Cave exploring in Southeast Asia has only begun. Spelunking, or speleology, has untold possibilities for the adventure traveler.

Chapter 5

RIVER EXPLORING
From Wild Rivers to Luxury Cruising

Which are the great rivers of Asia? The Yangtze? The Mekong? The Ganges? The Irrawaddy? There are others which, though they may not be as big, as long, or as world known, are by no means less exciting. Borneo has the Rejang, Malaysia the Endau and the Pahang, Thailand the Chao Phraya, and together Thailand, Laos, Cambodia and Vietnam share the Mekong. Even tiny Singapore has its Singapore River, all six miles of it.

People frown when I mention the Singapore River. But who has ever walked its full length and really gotten to know it? Not many. People complain nowadays that the river has been destroyed, that the old godowns and shophouses have been torn down, and that the colorful bumboats have disappeared. This is all true, but even when they were there, people took it all for granted and few people found time to explore the Singapore River.

By the same reasoning, this might apply to the other rivers of Southeast Asia. People don't have the time to get to know them, or appreciate them.

Take the Chao Phraya River, Thailand's main waterway that cuts through the very heart of the country and divides Bangkok into two cities. It may not be as long, nor perhaps as busy, as the Yangtze, or even the Mekong, but it ranks right alongside them in greatness. It's portrayed in photographs that appear on travel posters and book covers, in films and on billboards, in just about every medium that attempts to depict the exotic charm of the East. It's the Chao Phraya–with its endless fat rice barges in tow and the magnificent gold leaf temples lining the shores and glistening in the afternoon sun– that sells the Far East to the rest of the world.

But how many people know the river? I don't just mean visitors to Thailand but Bangkok residents, too. The river to most people is really an enigma, something they see from the terraces of five-star hotels or glance at when crossing a bridge. Until very recently, Bangkok had only one hotel on the river, and for a view of the river there are no wooded parks or vistas along its shores, nor is there even a mile of motorable road that parallel to its banks. The mood of the river has been kept a secret, to all but a few.

When I came to Bangkok some thirty years ago, my experiences with the river were no more than the occasional visit to the floating market when I wanted to show off the city to a visiting friend. The river was simply there, like a great picture window, but with the curtains always drawn. My curtains to the Chao Phraya opened quite unexpectedly. It happened when I arrived on the river from the sea, after sailing my schooner *Third Sea* up from Singapore.

We were in no hurry, and had spent many weeks anchored at various islands along the Malaysian and Thai coasts. For my reading aboard, I stashed away a number of good books. One was Joseph Conrad's *The Shadow Line,* which I read with keen interest while we were anchored in a small cove on the island of Ko Samui in southern Thailand. Sitting on deck under an awning, all I had to do was lift my eyes and look at a small fishing village on the shore, and there was Conrad's world, still.

A part of the passage that concerned me was the difficult sandbar at the mouth of the Chao Phraya, which we had to cross. The narrow channel through the bar is forever changing, and staying in its confined corridors can be a tricky business. When we picked up the first marker, many miles out at sea, and began working our way up the ranges, I suddenly felt as though I had done it all before. I then realized that I had, in the pages of *The Shadow Line*.

"One early morning we crossed the bar," Conrad wrote, "and while the sun was rising splendidly over the flat spaces of land, we steamed up the innumerable bends, passed the shadow of the great gilt pagoda, and reached the outskirts of town." It was unbelievable. Basically the river had not changed. It was exactly as Conrad had described it.

The "great gilt pagoda" he mentioned more than a hundred years ago is still there, only now, due to the shifting of the river, it is set back further from the main stream. But it's still a landmark, seen by every ship's captain and crew that passes up and down the river.

Conrad continued his description of the river and his approach to Bangkok: "There it was, spread largely on both banks, the Oriental capital which had yet suffered no white conqueror. Here and there in the distance, above the crowded mob of low, brown roof ridges, towered great piles of masonry, king's palaces, temples, gorgeous and dilapidated, crumbling under the vertical sunlight, tremendous, overpowering, almost palpable, which seemed to enter one's breast with the breath of one's nostrils and soak into one's ribs through every pore of one's skin."

In these terms, Joseph Conrad described his arrival in Bangkok on that bright morning of 24 January 1888. Were Joseph Conrad to return and sail that same river today, his descriptions would still be valid, and his feelings, I'm certain, would be the same. The river can do that for you.

For more than a year I lived aboard *Third Sea* on the Chao Phraya, down at the mouth near Samut Prakan. The river here is wide, and I was able to observe life on the river, for every vessel, large and small, entering or leaving Bangkok, had to pass before me. Vessels of every flag from every nation found their way past the gray-stoned Customs and Immigration Building. There were tankers and freighters, flat-bottomed scows and lighters, barges loaded with stone and charcoal, and others with rice, being towed by powerful tugs, river taxis and ferries, sampans being sculled, trim gigs from naval vessels, cruise boats, long long-tail skiffs clipping along at incredible speeds, even great sailing junks with their lug sails pulling hard on the quarter, and, last, the Thai fishing boats, by the thousands, coming and going with the tides, feeding a

59

hungry city with their 400 tons of fish every day, and each boat with its sea-toughened crew, torsos tattooed in enigmatic designs, all waving and laughing.

The best time to feel the mood is early morning. At first light, before dawn, the river is intimate. There is little movement, and one almost feels the presence of others as an intrusion. Blinding colors from a tropical sun have not yet supplanted soft grays, and uncertain forms on distant banks, the silhouette of trees or temple spires, that are harsh by day now loom soft in shades of coolness.

Then through the fog and mist rising up from the river, barges in tow, like elephants holding tails in a circus performance, slowly appear. Soon another string of barges come into sight, and another. A river taxi scurries across the water. A freighter lifts anchor and sounds its whistle. A sampan with sleepy-eyed ladies of the night hastily pulls away from a tanker which is also leaving, and now schoolchildren, all in neat scrubbed uniforms, arrive aboard a river bus. People wave and I have another cup of coffee on the aft deck. The river has come to life, pulsating, vibrant.

By mid-morning, Bangkok shimmers in the heat, and while the city swelters, the children born to the river take over. The wide expanse of brown water becomes their playground. Naked, with the image of innocence, they let themselves be dragged through the water by holding on to passing boats, they dive from piers and docksides, and some, the more daring, leap from the highest bridges into the swift currents below, only to come bobbing up a few feet downstream, their faces aglow with cherubic smiles.

Watching this life on the river is a delightful experience, and one soon realizes the exotic charms of the East are still present. Whenever I hear that someone has become disenchanted with the Orient, usually because the changes they have seen were too rapid, I often wonder if they have seen the Chao Phraya from water level. To do this you must forget the floating market tours and all the travel brochures. Hire a boat and be its master and cruise the main river and the labyrinth of canals. Unlike its counterpart in Italy, this tropical Venice bares its soul to the voyager, and doesn't hide it jealously behind stone facades or in museums.

The river has no time; it is ageless and it cannot be measured in any biblical span. Its source is the upper valleys of the north, where four major streams originate and flow south. They are the Ping, the Wang, the Yom and the Nan. They merge above Nakon Sawan to form the Chao Phraya. From Nakhon Sawan to the Gulf of Thailand, a distance of 212 miles, the river falls no more than nine feet. It flows slowly, and twice daily meets the incoming tides. It is this changing tide that governs the traffic flow on the river.

The port of Bangkok, with its main docks at Klong Toey, handles 90 percent of the country's imports. The biggest handicap to shipping is the silting up of the river at the mouth. Sedimentation extends the plain into the gulf at the rate of five to seven yards a year, and constant dredging of the bar is required to permit ships of more than 2,000 tons to cross. Dredging operations cost the government millions of dollars every year.

Small sailing craft in the past had it much easier than seagoing vessels today. The river then was navigable up to Ayutthaya, which was the center of the kingdom up until the 18th century. Chinese junks and Bugis traders made their way up the river to the old capital. The first Europeans to arrive were the Portuguese in 1511. They reported the Chinese had the monopoly on profitable trade in "rice, hides, tin, pepper, ebony and rosewood."

The Dutch began to arrive in 1605, followed by the Japanese in 1608. The Japanese were interested in procuring firearms and ammunition. In their opinion, Thai gunpowder was of surprisingly good quality. The first British ships anchored in Ayutthaya in 1612. The British East India Company set up a post in the same year.

In 1685, however, all trade with the West suddenly

stopped. The French, in a political maneuver, tried to place a Catholic convert on the throne. The king's first minister was executed, and thereafter, until the middle of the 19th Century, the kings of Siam discouraged commercial and diplomatic contacts with the West. Again, the only vessels on the Chao Phraya were Chinese and Thai junks. No European craft entered the river for 140 years.

After the fall of Ayutthaya to the Burmese, King Taksin moved his capital to Thonburi, and in 1782, the founder of the present dynasty, King Rama I, moved the capital from Thonburi across the river to its present location, then called "Village of the Wild Olive," better known as Bangkok.

The British East India Company began limited trade in 1826, but foreigners were forbidden to travel or remain ashore overnight. It wasn't until 1865 when King Mongkut made a treaty with Great Britain that gave "British subjects the right to trade and reside permanently in Bangkok." The door was opened; foreign vessels again appeared on the river. Soon afterwards, two sea captains opened a hotel in Bangkok for officers who wanted to spend time ashore, and they called it the Oriental Hotel. It still stands, Bangkok's oldest, and the first hotel on the river. Before the Sathorn Bridge was erected down river from the Oriental, I anchored my schooner out from the hotel. I had the same splendid view Conrad had when he took command of the *Otega,* which was also anchored in front of the Oriental.

The old Protestant cemetery in New Road, near the night market, bears testimony to some of the early seafarers who were destined to change the course of Thailand's history. Captain John Brush was one. King Rama IV appointed him harbor master and ordered him to build the present lighthouse at Paknam. Captain Bush was also the first foreigner to serve in the Royal Thai Navy, and when King Rama IV visited Singapore and Indonesia in 1870, he chose Captain Bush to accompany him.

Captain Bush spent 38 years with the Thai Navy. In

memory of his service, Bush Lane, which leads from New Road to the new Royal Orchid Hotel on the river, was named in his honor. The hotel has also paid tribute to Captain Bush by naming its main restaurant after him.

And, of course, an early sailor who came up river and left his mark was Joseph Conrad. A sea captain then, he later turned novelist after failing health took him from the sea that he loved so much. Conrad and other writers who followed him tell the story of the river from the late 19th century onwards.

Many European structures from the late 19th and early 20th centuries can still be seen along the right bank of the river in the vicinity of the Oriental Hotel. Here Europeans built their legations and their major houses, along with churches and private residences which served the foreign community. Of all these former legations along the river, only the Portuguese and French remain. These can be seen not far from the Oriental Hotel.

Even Conrad in his time was witness to some of the changes that were taking place back then in Bangkok. He tells us about his travels by horse-drawn carriage, and he complains about the city that's overrun with rickshaws. Only a few years before he arrived, a Chinese nobleman humbly presented a rickshaw to the king for his private use. By Conrad's time the vehicle existed in such large numbers that the government had to promulgate an act governing its use. The reason cited was public safety.

Thailand is one country in Asia that has done much to preserve its heritage. Its Royal Barge Procession on the Chao Phraya is one example. The tradition, preserved down through the ages, is for the king at the end of the rainy season to make his royal *kathin,* which means bringing robes and gifts by river from the Grand Palace to the monks of Wat Arun. It is a splendid, colorful procession, that marks the climax to anyone's visit to Asia. The king sits on a throne in the largest barge in the procession, and there are dozens of them, all elegantly carved and gold-leafed, with the prows, gilded birds' heads, jutting proudly into the air. More than forty yards long, the king's barge requires a crew of 54 oarsmen, two steersmen, two officers, one flagman, and rhythm-keeper or drummer, and one singer who chants to the cadence of the oars. Other barges, although smaller, are no less impressive.

Although rickshaws, electric trams, horse drawn carriages and steamboats that operated on the klong are gone (due to the increase in traffic, many of the klongs have been filled in to make room for new roads and to widen older ones), Bangkok is still basically a water town. To feel the pulse beat of the city, all one need do is cruise the river, whether it be aboard a luxury hotel cruiser, a speeding long-tail ferry or the Chao Phraya River Express. A rewarding voyage is an overnight cruise aboard the luxury *Manohra Song*, a 40-year old restored rice barge. This is one way to feel the river, at dusk and at dawn, while moored alongside an ancient golden temple far up river, away from the hustle of Bangkok.

At the opposite extreme of the Chao Phraya is the Rejang River in Borneo. The Rejang is a wild river where fierce head-hunters once roamed. Headhunting has been outlawed, but you

The author with his wife Michelle and son Paul aboard Manohra Song, a luxury converted rice barge, on a weekend cruise to Ayutthaya, the former capital of Siam.

hear tales occasionally about a head being taken, as they were during World War II and the Indonesian Confrontation in 1964. Ibans today no longer hunt for heads, are usually friendly and don't mind visitors. As they had in the past, they continue to live in longhouses along the river.

The Rejang River to this day spells adventure. In the late 1960s, when Indonesia's internal struggles appeared to be coming to a close, I took the opportunity to explore the headwaters of the Rejang, and later, when I had my own schooner, I sailed up the Rejang to Kapit. Both trips were unforgettable experiences.

When I set out to explore the headwaters, my plan was to hire longboats in Kapit, the last outpost on the Rejang, and travel up river to where the Rejang meets the Balleh River. I would then follow the Balleh to its very source, leave the boat and hire porters, and cross into Kalimantan in Indonesia. That was my plan, but it didn't work out quite that way.

For the trip, I teamed up with Willy Mettler, a Swiss photographer who disappeared a few years later in the jungle of Cambodia. In Singapore, Willy and I purchased our supplies, loaded them aboard a Straits Steamship freighter and sailed to Kuching, the capital of Sarawak. In Kuching we picked up maps and shipped our supplies by boat to Kapit, some 180 miles from the mouth of the Rejang. The express launch was our first taste of river travel in Borneo.

The entire bottom of the launch was constructed of reinforced steel plate, and for a definite purpose. The Rejang is a highway for the timber industry. Rafts with as many as 200 logs float down stream, and occasionally logs break away from the rafts. When they do, and are left to themselves, they often become waterlogged and are hard to see from a launch speeding at fifteen to twenty-five miles an hour. When our launch hit the first log, I thought we were doomed, until I realized what had happened. The launch merely shuddered and shook and bounced over the log. We crashed over dozens of more logs before reaching Kapit.

Most of the fellow passengers were Ibans, returning to their longhouses. Ibans belong to but one of a dozen tribes in northern Borneo. Kayans and Kenyahs live in longhouses, like the Ibans do, but Punans are nomadic and dwell in small families in the jungle. At first, Willy and I found it difficult telling one tribe member from another, but after a few days we could recognize one from the other, with the exception of Punans. We had yet to meet our first Punan. That would come.

By late evening we reached Kapit, built high on a river bank. The town at that time had six miles of roads and five automobiles — and traffic problems! It was amazing what five cars can do when they all came to town at once, when the boat from down river arrives.

To the people who live up river, Kapit is their London, their Paris. It has electric lights, shops, and two cinemas. I was surprised to find that one cinema had a rather recent movie advertised on the posters outside. With time to spare, Willy and I bought tickets and went inside, only to find it was not the same movie as advertised. No one seemed to mind.

That night we stayed at the Kapit Hotel, our last bit of luxury for some time to come, and early the next morning we went to the shops along the river to negotiate for long-boats to carry us up river. Luck was with us. The Iban chief of Ruma Dilang, a longhouse near the mouth of the Balleh, invited us to travel with him and his family in their longboat. We could spend the night in his longhouse. We didn't have the chance to refuse, for instantly a dozen natives picked up our supplies and carted them down to the waterfront to be loaded into the boat.

When I saw the boat, I wasn't too sure we would make it. The frail craft was hollowed from a single tree trunk, and after we were seated, a dozen of us, it had only an inch or two of freeboard above the waterline.

The boat was about thirty feet long, propelled by a twenty-horsepower outboard motor. A young Iban boy who served as lookout sat on the bow. The helmsman sat in the stern and interpreted the arm signals from the boy in front. They threw off the mooring lines and we drifted out into the current. The helmsman cranked up the engine and nosed the bow upstream. He then gave it full throttle. The boat lunged forward and appeared to leap out of the water.

We moved like a surfboard over the swirling water. The bow rode high and the river hissed and slapped beneath us. It was exciting, but also a bit frightening at times. Half submerged logs appeared suddenly. The lookout would signal and the helmsman would turn, just in time.

We left the Rejang and started up the Balleh. In places it was as wide as a lake. We arrived at Ruma Dilang at dusk. As our supplies were being unloaded and carried up the mud banks, a servant from the chief's quarters came to lead us to the longhouse.

Borneo longhouses are truly primitive masterpieces of architecture. They are constructed entirely of wood, high off the ground on pilings and may stretch as far as half a mile from end to end. Some may house as many as 100 families, or 600 residents. A longhouse is actually a village under one roof.

The Rajang River is the life and soul, and the pulse beat, of Sawarak in Borneo. Life on the river is slow and sees little change. River boats, that carry both cargo and passengers, travel upriver to Kapit, the last outpost.

67

In bygone days it served as an armed fort against invading headhunting neighbors.

We were led to the chief's quarters in the very center of the house. The chief bade us sit on mats laid out for us. A boy who had some knowledge of English served as our interpreter and sat between Willy and me. When we were settled, two young girls took positions and sat directly in front us. They smiled and stared directly at us, as though they were ready to play some game. What was going to happen? The chief raised his hand for everyone to be quiet. He then made a short speech to which his people listened intently.

Flickering shadows from the oil lamps gave the place an eerie feeling. And occasionally came a strange sound and all conversation stopped for a moment. I looked over at Willy. His jaw was half open: he was staring blankly at something overhead. Along a ceiling beam hung tufts of straw. There appeared to be rice drying, but when I looked again I saw, half hidden among the straw, the fleshless forms of human heads.

Finally, the chief clapped his hands and several women appeared carrying bottles of strong rice wine called *tuak*. As we soon discovered, the duty of the girls in front of us was to make sure we didn't get thirsty. The girl facing me lifted a glass of wine and held it towards me. When I took hold of it, she maintained her grip and forced it to my lips. After I had taken a few gulps, and wanted to stop, she kept pouring it down my throat, until the glass was empty. Tears poured downed my cheeks and my throat burned as though I had swallowed hot coals. Before I could recover, she refilled my glass and repeated the process. Somehow, after the second glass, the heads hanging above us no longer mattered.

Natives from other quarters came to form a circle around us. Someone began chanting and several youths picked up the beat and started pounding on log drums. An old lady with sagging breasts and a toothless grin staggered to her feet and did a hip-swinging dance. The crowd broke into laughter. A few other tipsy women got up and did a short dance. Our girl attendants poured more *tuak*. We laughed with the others, and even tried our luck at dancing but it was difficult to maintain a balance. By midnight, everyone, from the chief down, was in a state of complete intoxication. With the party still going, I laid my head against a post. The night fused into a dream.

Dawn came lighting up the verandah in a reddish glow, and I was again aware of heads hanging above. Ibans were noted for being the most wicked headhunters in Borneo, if not in all the world. Headhunting among all the island tribes was once a national sport. An Iban maiden would not accept the advances of a young man unless he had taken a head in battle.

Later that morning, we found several boats about to travel upstream, and their owners agreed to carry us and our supplies for barter goods we had for the occasion. As we were to discover, finding transportation on the river would be no problem, nor would it be difficult to put up for the night in a longhouse. We were always welcome, and our presence was always an excuse for a celebration. Several days later, we reached the last longhouse on the Balleh River. It was a splendid house, and one so vast I could not see from one end

Human skulls hanging in a longhouse on the Rajang River in Sawarak. Head hunting was outlawed by the British, but occasionally a head may fall, as happened during World War II. Right, Stephens on a log raft on the Rajang.

to the other. Over *tuak* we negotiated for two longboats and eight porters to guide us and carry our supplies into Kalimantan. With the deal sealed, and a few more strong *tuaks,* Willy and I feigned drunkenness and got to sleep while the party was still in full swing. Early the next morning, with blurry-eyed boatmen and porters, we set out for the headwaters.

The jungle became a mass of tangled vegetation. The forest hung far over the muddy river and it was impossible to see the river banks. Occasionally we came to an island that divided the river and here the waters always ran swift and deep. There were fewer long rafts floating down stream and we no longer saw longboats or dugouts. We were entering no man's land.

For safety we slept in the longboats which we moored to tree branches hanging over the water. Our diet was mainly boiled rice and tinned beef, although occasionally the Ibans gathered jungle fruit from the forest.

When the river shallowed, we abandoned our boats and took to the jungle on foot. After the first day, our Iban guides began acting strangely. We didn't know it at the time, but Ibans fear the jungle Punans, and we were in Punan territory.

Seldom does one ever see a Punan in the jungle, but they are there. We began to imagine eyes following us. Our convictions became a fact one evening. We had set up camp along a steep slope. The Ibans were gathering firewood and preparing for the night; Willy and I were setting up our lean-tos. Suddenly a Punan materialized out of the jungle and stood at the edge of the clearing, in the semidarkness of the forest. He was very dark, almost black, and wore nothing but a loincloth. He stood motionless. His black hair hung down his back and was tied at the end. Like a shepherd holding his staff, he clung to a blow pipe that towered several inches above his head. His piercing stare froze our Iban guides where they stood.

Then, like a statue coming to life, the lone Punan sprang into motion. With an effortless movement he scaled the steep embankment and in an instant was gone. He needed to utter no words of warning that we were treading in his forbidden territory. I fell asleep not knowing what to expect.

The next morning I awoke to find our camp was deathly still. I sat up and nudged Willy. We slowly stuck our heads out of the lean-to. The camp was deserted. Our tribesmen had abandoned us, leaving us with all our supplies.

It would take several more days to reach Kilimantan, a journey we could probably not make without a guide. Nor could we carry the necessary supplies. We had no alterative but to retrace our steps and return to Kapit via the Balleh. Losing no time, we packed up what supplies we could carry and set out for the Balleh.

We saw no other Punans but we were certain they were there, following our progress. We didn't know if we would meet with a poison dart or if they might give us a helping hand if the need arose. It was an eerie feeling to know you are being watched without being able to detect those doing the watching.

We had little trouble retracing our steps. Had we been in flat country, we might have been lost forever, but now we had small streams to follow that eventually lead us into the Balleh.

Once we reached the river we were in luck. A timber crew had tied a dozen logs together to form a raft which was moored in the still waters to a tree along the bank. We threw the few supplies we had left aboard, cut the mooring line and poled our raft out into the current, bound for Kapit.

For the next several days, the raft became our home. In the afternoons we napped in the warm sun, and when it became too warm, we held on to a twisted vine rope and dragged from the stern in the cool water. We listened to the jungle and watched fish jump in the river. But there were also frightening moments when we came upon rapids. The first day out, we were eating a tin of bully beef for lunch when I happened to look up. The water ahead was swirling like an automatic washing machine and we were heading toward an island of jagged rocks at midstream. We met the rapids head on. The logs beneath us twisted and turned and pulled at the taut vines that held the raft together. Any second I expected the raft to splinter and pile up like a box of matches dumped on a table top.

But the raft held and we safely passed the rapids without incident. After that, an occasional rapid now and then broke the monotony. When we reached longhouses further down river, women bathing and washing clothes in the stream did double-takes as they watched us slowly drift by.

On the fifth day we ran upon a sand bank at Ramah Temonggong Jugah. A longboat with an outboard picked us up and we transferred to a Chinese trading boat. The next day we reached Kapit.

Years later I did return to the Rejang with my schooner *Third Sea*. On that second trip, I gained sympathy and respect for another yachtsman, a man who had made his way up the river a hundred years before. He was James Brooke. While I was able to motor up river to reach Kapit, Captain Brooke, having no engine, had to make way up river by sail alone. But then, James Brooke had turned his trip into a romance that Southeast Asia has never been able to live down. James quelled a rebellion, and became the first White Raja of Sarawak, a rank held by him and his offspring until World War II, when Sabah and Sarawak became part of Malaysia.

Another river I truly enjoy traveling on is the Irrawaddy in Burma. Paddle-wheel river boats negotiate the river on scheduled routes, and it's possible to rent a cabin aboard one of the vessels and a spend week cruising up river to Mandalay and beyond.

Chapter 6

MOTORING AND FOUR-WHEEL DRIVE SAFARIS
Driving Main Roads and Back Roads

Thirty years ago, a race car driver succeeded in setting a record for driving from Singapore to Bangkok in less than 30 hours. He made the run in 29 hours and 32 minutes. At the time, it was considered an incredible feat.

But back then, in the late 1960s, it wasn't an easy thing to do, even without trying to break records. The odds were stacked against anyone going the distance without a mishap. The route covered a grueling 897 miles, much of it over potted, unpaved roads, across unbridged rivers and through rough jungle terrain. The most difficult section was in southern Thailand. Malaysia was somewhat better; it had what they called a 'trunk' road left over from the British days. In Thailand the road was mostly unpaved, crowded with timber lorries, and it wound its way through rugged mountainous terrain. There were few gasoline stations and even fewer garages. Motorists had to contend with monsoon rains, floods and cattle on the road, and if the driving conditions didn't get them, the bandits might. Muslim rebels in the south in those days were always holding up cars and buses, and from time to time even the Bangkok-Singapore Express train.

And there was always the unexpected. Motorists often complained about one stretch of road in southern Thailand when stray herds of elephants often blocked the way.

The same year the record was set for the drive from Singapore to Bangkok, I took a four-wheel drive vehicle and made the drive from Bangkok to Chiang Rai, and back to Bangkok. The trip took a grueling eight days, which included sitting behind the driver's wheel twelve hours at a time. The drive from Chiang Rai to Fang alone took three days. The biggest delay was fording rivers and streams. In one 36-mile stretch we counted 22 streams. In some streams where a mud bottom was threatening, the Thais lined the bottom with rolls of matted bamboo. More tires were punctured this way, but at least you didn't get stuck. And when it wasn't raining, the dust was unbearable. It got into everything.

After Thailand, I motored down the Malay Peninsula to Singapore. It took six days, again driving 12 hours a day.

Today, 30 years later, it's a different story. Not too long ago, I did the drive with a friend in his Mercedes from Singapore to Bangkok; we made it in an easy three days, all during daylight driving. The roads were paved all the way, and some had been turned into super highways, with cloverleaves and overpasses.

Oftentimes when I want to visit Chiang Mai, and I'm not in a rush, I drive. I rent an Avis car and make the trip from Bangkok to the northern city in a leisurely one day drive. Sometimes I stop in route, perhaps at Ayutthaya or maybe Lamphun, and then it takes two days. The nice thing about it, I can hop on a Thai Airways flight back to Bangkok when I reach Chiang Mai. There's no hassle getting to and from airports. Avis has an airport check-in service.

Driving is undoubtedly one of the best ways to see a country. Yet every time I mention that I might be driving to Chiang Mai, or down south to Surat Thani or Songkhla, and maybe

Getting off the main road may require a four-wheel drive vehicle, as seen here. The author crossing a stream in a Land Cruiser in Thailand.

Singapore, I get the same reaction from everyone—"You're driving! You gotta be mad." I hate to tell people, but in recent years I drove between Singapore and Bangkok a half dozen times. I love the drive.

When you look at a road map of Southeast Asia, you wonder if these people might not be right. The landscape is made up of some really diverse terrain. Literally there are thousands of miles of roads that traverse mountain ranges, cut through dense verdant jungles, skirt past endless miles of lonely beaches and lead to big cities and small villages alike.

Obstacles that I had to face 30 years ago are fewer. It's rare to see wild elephants crossing the road and seldom do we see water buffalo grazing along the road sides. And fortunately, bandits and rebel insurgents no longer come down from the hills to rob people. They are probably engaged in the tourist trade. It's more profitable.

There are today new highways from the southern tip of the Malay Peninsula to the northern reaches of Thailand, with modern petrol stations, restaurants and rest stops every few miles. That race car driver who broke the record 30 years ago would have no difficulty were he attempting to cover the route in less than 30 hours these days. If he left Singapore a few hours before dawn, he could be in Bangkok at midnight the same day. No long lunch breaks, though.

But speed should not be our quest. The objective should be to take advantage of the new roads and at the same time to take in the sights.

Which brings up another complaint I often hear—that all these modern highways make driving monotonous. On the contrary, the highways have added another dimension to motoring. They have opened up whole new vistas that motorists before never saw.

In the past, drivers were preoccupied keeping their eyes focused on the road, and what views they did have were usually blocked by jungle landscape and heavy foliage. It was a case of not being able to see the forest for the trees.

Not all countries in Southeast Asia, however, are suitable for getting behind the driver's wheel and taking off. I am talking about three countries—Thailand, Malaysia and Singapore. The other ASEAN countries should be approached with caution, if at all. Cambodia is definitely out, and Indonesia is debatable, unless driving is confined to tourist spots, like Bali. The same goes for the Philippines. I have rented cars in Manila and driven down the Bataan Peninsula, and again in Cebu, but that is about the limit. Hiring a chauffeured car is something else.

When people look at the traffic congestion in the capital cities—Singapore, Kuala Lumpur and Bangkok—the first thought that comes to mind is that they could never drive in these conditions. But once you leave these metropolitan areas, the picture changes.

The whole idea behind self driving is to explore. Signs along the highway point the way to towns and villages. Both Malaysia and Thailand are lands of discovery, and discovery means getting off the beaten path. It takes a bit of exploring to fully enjoy a motor trip. To find your way around, there are some very fine road maps on the market. When motoring in Thailand, choose a map that is written in Thai script as

Thirty years ago it took the author five days, and many streams to ford, to drive across northern Thailand. Today it can be covered in a day.

well as in English, unless, of course, you know Thai. It does help. Whenever I am driving a back road in Thailand and find that I am lost, it is very easy to point to the map and ask a local for directions.

Accommodations anywhere throughout Thailand are plentiful, and adequate. When you are behind the driver's wheel, you can pick and choose. Nor do you need to worry about reservations.

Let's first look at motoring in Thailand. Heading southwest from Bangkok, to either the Malaysia border or to Phuket, the motorist has the choice of three routes. The eastern route is the road that follows the Gulf of Thailand, past Songkhla, Pattani and Narathiwat. When I am driving to Malaysia I take this route. It is slower but very enjoyable. There is practically no traffic and the motorist always has a pleasant view of the sea to one side and the bluish-gray mountains in the interior on the other. Short drives on back roads into the mountains are possible.

The second alternative is the central road, often called by old timers "the trunk road." It is the one most used, and thus has the most traffic. The road leads through the town of Trang, a tourist destination that has just opened up.

Highways may be paved in Southeast Asia but wild elephants still cross the roads, as this sign indicates. Photo by Robert Stedman.

The third road follows in sight of the Burma border and leads to Phuket. A causeway connect Phuket to the mainland, thus making driving onto the island possible. And Phuket is a great island to explore behind the driver's wheel.

All three roads have interesting sights along the way — fishing ports, mountain temples, limestone caves, waterfalls and wilderness parks, all listed on tourist maps.

A drive I enjoy taking is to the east of Bangkok towards Tongchai Prasat. The road skirts the northern border of Cambodia and leads to southern Laos. For those who love to visit Khmer ruins, this is the road to take. There are literally dozens of ruins, some as big as a village, and others the size of a city block. Recently I drove with a friend in his car right up to the Laos border. We parked on the Thai side, walked across the border and went by bus to the ruins at Wat Phu near Pakse. We could have driven into Laos but after seeing the deeply rutted roads, I was glad that we didn't.

When you look at a map of Thailand, you will notice the main roads are marked in red, and the smaller minor roads are in black. You may wonder what these back roads might be like—rough, half paved, pot holed. On the contrary, I've found that even the roads marked in black are very serviceable roads. Not only serviceable, they are usually the most beautiful, and interesting. Along these roads you might find a cave to explore, or a lovely Thai temple to photograph, or as I mentioned, a Khmer ruin. Not all the sites are listed on tourist brochures or road maps, however.

Even the smallest village can be interesting. There are food shops and most likely a hotel or two. One thing for certain, there will be no graffiti, and pollution is almost nonexistent.

Thailand is a large country, and customs and traditions change from north to south. Architecture included. In the north, construction is mostly wood; in the south it's concrete. The farther south you drive, the more prevalent becomes the Muslim influence. Windows in homes take on the shape of onion domes and mosques replace temples. Women dress in traditional Muslim dress. In some towns you swear your are in Malaysia.

Northern Thailand has an excellent network of highways, well marked with signs in English. As I mentioned, Chiang Mai is an easy one-day drive. The roads to the northeast also lead to some interesting discoveries, such as Ban Chang, pottery sites that predate anything in Europe and the Middle East.

In the far corners of Thailand's northwest there are still very few roads, and here I would suggest another adventure — a four-wheel drive safari. Here you leave the driving up to someone else. Until fairly recently, travel in this area through hilltribe villages and dense jungle was only possible on horse or elephant, or on foot. Today, thanks to companies like Royal Orchid Holidays that provide vehicles as well as drivers, isolated communities can be reached by four-wheel drive. A drive through the rugged terrain, mostly along dirt tracks, is the ideal way to see the spectacular scenery of forests and hills and previously inaccessible hilltribe settlements, and to reach rafting and hiking trails.

One of the best trails leads from the northern capital, Chiang Mai, to Pai District in Mae Hong Son, winding through forests, elephant working camps, hilltribe villages and many natural wonders.

Let us turn south once more and this time cross the border from Thailand into Malaysia. Since we can't cross borders in rental cars, the best way to do a self-drive trip through Malaysia is to fly from Thailand to Penang and rent a car there.

When you look at a road map of Malaysia it appears big, and it is; but there's no one place in the country that's more than a day's drive from Kuala Lumpur. The reason is Malaysia has an excellent network of roads. They traverse some fantastically beautiful countryside, climb to soaring mountain peaks, cut through dense verdant jungles, skirt past endless miles of lonely beaches and lead to big city and small kampong alike.

Accommodations, as in Thailand, are good, with everything from Swiss type chalets in hidden mountain retreats to palm thatched cottages at remote beach resorts. And aside from hotels, which are everywhere, there are a few government resthouses still left. Resthouses are hangovers from the British Raj when the government furnished resthouses — in India they call them dak bungalows–over 20 miles, the distant one could travel on a bullock cart.

There's the new super highway that I mentioned, from Jahore across from Singapore in the south up the central plateau to the border of Thailand. But we're not in a hurry. Let's explore, and take the back roads. Suppose, for example, you are in Kuala Lumpur and want to drive to Malacca, the port captured by the Portuguese in 1507. There's a super highway that leads from the capital almost to Malacca's city limits, but there's also a back road through rubber plantations and oil palm estates, past an old lighthouse at Port Dickson, and through a village where there are huge stone carvings dating back to the early voyages of the Phoenicians some 2,000 years ago. In most cases, back roads will prove to be the most interesting.

I might mention, the old road to Malacca from Port Dickson leads through some of the most picturesque kampongs, or villages, in all Malaysia. Kampong houses are built high off the ground on stilts, usually with stone stairways leading to the living quarters on the upper level. A few of the high, steep roofs are tin, but most are traditional attap. Malays take great pride in their kampong houses.

Motorists in Malaysia find that hill stations provide a very different experience. Within easy driving distance from Kuala Lumpur are a number of cool mountain retreats, or hill stations, as they are generally called. Sweaters and warming fireplaces instead of bikinis and suntans. A game of golf above the clouds in place of water skiing. Exhilarating fresh air, strolling along a mountain path, awe inspiring views of verdant valleys below and rolling green mountains beyond. Or it might even be sitting down at a table with a stack of chips in front of you, placing bets at the roulette wheel. It's all part of Malaysia's hill stations, and all depends upon what pleasures you seek.

The closest hill station to the capital is Fraser's Hill, only a few hours' drive. Like Rome, it is built on seven hills. The station got its name from Louis James Fraser, a rogue who ran an Old West style mule train over the mountain range a hundred years ago. Fraser's Hill was a favorite retreat for expat British rubber planters before the war.

The largest and certainly most famous of these mountain retreats is Cameron Highlands, the resort where American Jim Thompson, the Thai Silk king, disappeared and was never seen again. But don't let this throw you off. There were motives for his disappearance other than simply getting lost. The 50-mile drive from the main road to the resort is mountainous and passes through some beautiful tropical rain forests, in view of aborigine villages.

A road leads to Maxwell Hill, the northernmost hill station, but the only access is by government owned and operated Land Rovers. There is a safe parking lot for private cars at the foot of the hill. Land Rovers depart every 30 minutes. Maxwell Hill is the least known of all hill stations.

One drive in Malaysia that is suited for the motorist is the East Coast. For a distance of 138 miles, from Kuantan to Trengganu, a two-lane road follows a very lovely and picturesque coastline. It's also along this stretch of countryside where grown men fly kites and spin tops, where villagers worship at the grave of a mermaid, where turtles nine feet long come up the beach to lay their eggs, and where there are interesting fishing villages to explore.

Life is tranquil and unspoiled. Tropical beaches, palm fringed and washed by the warm waters of the South China Sea stretch for endless, unbroken miles along the coast. Prahus with triangular sails glide lazily across calm seas and kampongs with fishing nets hung up to dry add touches of charm and serenity to the scene. The East Coast makes every traveler wish he were an artist.

The last major town on the East Coast is Kota Bharu. Being close to the Thai border, signs on shops are printed in both Thai and Malay and most of the local people speak both languages.

One attraction of Kota Bharu is the beach that lies seven miles to the north. It's called Pantai Chinta Berahi, or the Beach of Passionate Love. Ironically, it was here that the Japanese landed during the opening days of World War II. A few pillboxes on the beach are grim reminders of the past.

A complaint many motorists had about driving up the East Coast was that the road deadended at KB and they had to return by the same route. No more. There is a new modern highway that connects the East Coast with Penang in the west. It's a breathtaking drive across the tops of the mountain chain that runs from Thailand down the peninsula to Singapore. Where motorists once had to drive south to make the crossing from one side of the peninsula to the other, usually a two-day trip, it can be made via the new highway, in four or five hours.

Motorists driving from Kuala Lumpur to Penang and points north usually take the super highway, and make the journey in six hours. There is an alternative route that hugs the coastline and is much more interesting. The motorist leaves

Mosque at Kuala Kangsar in Malaysia. Photo by Robert Stedman.

Kuala Lumpur via the double lane highway to Klang, the Royal Town, and then follows the signs to Kuala Selangor and Telok Anson. The drive is through rural Malaysia. There are countless small kampongs and tiny fishing villages that spur off from the main road to the sea. Much of the area is delta land, situated at the mouths of rivers, and there are ferry crossings to make and bridges to cross.

Telok Anson is the biggest town along the route. It's a quiet town, with a central plaza and a clock tower, and although it's far up river it continues to be an important trading center. Barges and flat bottom scows tie up along the river waterfront where they load and unload their wares. Back to the trunk road, there's a turn off that points to Kuala Kangsar.

For those who want to stick to the main road, there are some interesting sights. Seven miles north of Kuala Lumpur are the famous Batu Caves, center of the yearly Hindu Festival of Thaipusam which we have seen in the chapter "Spelunking vs. Speleology."

Another interesting drive is to take the mountain road beyond Batu Caves to Lake Chini in the very heart of the Malay Peninsula. Unlike the past when I had to camp on the side of the lake, with leeches and mosquitoes for company, today the lake had been transformed into a resort area of sorts

The ferry from Butterworth to Penang. Photo by Robert Stedman.

with lovely chalets and boats to take visitors on cruises around the lake. Guides will be quick to tell you that beneath the lake is a lost city, and that a sea monster lives in the lake.

Caves and limestone outcroppings are a main feature of the Malaysian countryside. The motorists traveling from one end of the peninsula to the other will see these strange phenomena, rising up perpendicular from the jungle floor. Many are merely shells, with deep caves and caverns within. It was in caves like these on the Malay Peninsula that early man sought refuge some 10,000 years ago. With the building craze that is going in Malaysia, many of the outcroppings are being mined for their limestone that is used to make cement. Some hills have been completely leveled. Even the famous Batu Caves was doomed to extinction until a few years ago when the government stopped mining concessions on the mountain.

A few miles off the main road is Kuala Kangsar. It has an excellent rest house high on the banks of the Perak River and some very worthwhile sights. The Ubudiah Mosque with its great golden dome is one of the finest mosques on this side of the world. With permission it's possible to visit the Sultan's Palace, and nearby is a splendid "old palace" called the Ceremonial House. It's a grand old timber building on stilts with elaborate gingerbread decorations. It could pass for a house in the Russian Crimea.

A scene that always impresses the foreigner in Malaysia, especially those traveling by automobile for any distance, are the endless forests of rubber trees. Forty percent of the world's natural rubber comes from Malaysia, which means a lot of trees. Yet in comparison to other well established industries, rubber production is relatively new. As an experiment, the first rubber trees were sent out from England to Singapore in the late 1880's, but no one took rubber growing seriously. An Englishman named Ridgley carried seven rubber tree seedlings to Kuala Kangsar to plant in the botanical gardens there. Then, almost overnight, the trees that Ridgley couldn't give away were in demand. It happened when James Dunlop invented the pneumatic tire, and soon after Malaya had a new multimillion dollar industry.

Motorists shooting through the Malaysian countryside may wonder why there never seems to be much activity in a rubber forest. The neat rows of trees always appear void of people. The reason is that the rubber tapper's day is over by the time most people are stirring in the morning. He usually begins his day at 3:00 AM and by breakfast the latex is gathered and sent to sheds for processing into sheets. Motorists have the advantage of being able to visit any of the plantations and watch rubber being processed. Managers are usually pleased to show visitors around, since few ever stop.

Also along the road north from Kuala Lumpur the motorist will notice huge tin dredging mines. Unlike the rubber plantations, visitors are cautioned to stay clear. Tin mines with their uncertain wooden scaffolding can be dangerous. But don't hesitate to stop and study one up close. There are several methods of mining tin. The open cast mine is the most commonly seen from the road. The huge power jets of water are breaking down the tin-rich soil which is then lifted by either gravel pumps or hydraulic elevators to the dredgers where the ore is removed. Usually at many open cast mines tin panners can be seen, knee deep in sludge, swirling a large circular pan about in front of them. In early times all tin deposits were worked this way.

Beyond Kuala Kangsar is a quiet charming town, Taiping. It has a very good rest house and a hotel facing the Lake Gardens. Its museum is the oldest in the country with a fine collection of ancient weapons and some rather seedy-looking archaeological findings. Taiping is also the gateway to Maxwell Hill, six miles away. If you plan to visit the hill station, the last government owned and operated Landrover that serves as a bus up the hill (no private automobiles) departs at 6:30 PM. If you have left reservations to the last minute, the attendant at the gate will phone ahead and inform you if there are rooms available.

The island of Penang is one of the biggest tourist spots in Southeast Asia. It's a duty-free port with much to see and do, and the motorist has advantages over the general tourist. With your own automobile there are places to discover. Certainly recommended is a drive around the island. Visit the temples, like the Snake Temple, and explore the beaches to the north. But also get off the beaten track. Don't be afraid to follow roads that leave the main road, many which will deadend at the sea, but lead you to forgotten fishing villages.

A car ferry connects Penang with the mainland. The ferries run often, take twenty minutes, and a fee is charged only on the return voyage. The nighttime approach to Penang by ferry is an exciting experience. The island has no docks, so trading vessels—tramp steamers, seagoing junks, freighters, cruise vessels, tankers—all anchor in the straits. All through the night the lights of scows and barges ply the waterways, back and forth from wharf to ship.

Unless travelers are journeying to Bangkok, few ever venture north of Penang. Although there is no highly geared tourist industry in the area, there are two of Malaysia's most picturesque states that are worth visiting: Kedah and the pocket-size Perlis of only 316 square miles.

The earliest known trade with the West came through Kedah and Perlis. A Neolithic site in Perlis has yielded Greek pottery dating back to the 4th Century B.C. Malaysia reached a high state of culture in Kedah with strong Hindu ties.

Motorists who begin their journey in Penang might want to make a one-day excursion to visit Kedah and Perlis, or for those who want to linger longer, there are rest houses in Alor Star, Baling, Sungei Patani, Kulim and on Langkawi, the group of legendary islands off the coast. These two important rice-growing states were once part of old Siam, which is Thailand today. Thai is the spoken language as well as Malay.

The road to the north of Alor Star leads to the Thai border at Padang Besar, a road-rail frontier town.

From the Penang ferry landing at Butterworth the road to the north passes through several miles of deserted Australian military camps to Sungei Patani. The town was once a famous site, the starting point of the great elephant trail that led across the peninsula. As mentioned earlier in Chapter 3, vessels unloaded cargo on the East Coast and transported it overland to the Indian Ocean, thus avoiding the pirate-infested Straits of Malacca. The trade route dates back some 2,000 years.

The road continues north to Alor Star, the state capital and royal town. Worth visiting here are the Balai Besar and Balai Nobat, and the famous black dome Tahir Mosque. The hiking enthusiast might find the 4,000 feet Kedah Peak an interesting climb. It's close to Alor Star on the Sungei Pantani Road.

One of the greatest discoveries in the north is the Langkawi Islands. Here truly is the last paradise.

The islands—there are 93 in the group—are located 20 miles off the coast along the Thai border. From a distance they appear as one, spread out along the horizon in a jagged silhouette. But as your ferry closes the distance the aspect changes. Cliffs drop abruptly into the sea and form narrow waterways that divide and subdivide the land into countless smaller islands.

The ferry passes through these channels. Some cliffs are solid masses of marble, while others are serrated quartz and granite. More islands and passageways appear. It becomes a labyrinth. It's obvious now why pirates and buccaneers of old used the Langkawis as their refuge. No man-of-war could possibly hunt them down.

The ferry edges through the last channel and granite cliffs give way to a sweeping curve of a bay. Fishing boats are anchored on still waters. Rows of houses set back from the beach are nestled among clusters of palms. A concrete jetty reaches out into the bay. The place is Pekan Kuah, the main village.

Gone, of course, are the rambunctious days of pirates,

but the islands continue to lure wayward travelers looking for a refuge from our modern hurried world. Few places can be so remote and yet so near. Few places can have so much and yet so little to offer.

There are few amenities for the tourist, but enough to make a stay enjoyable, if luxury isn't the quest. Pekan Kuah has a rest house, hotels, a post office, and a few shops that sell batik, post cards and film. There is no bank, so it's advisable to carry currency in small denominations.

New hotels and inns, located by the sea, are modern and comfortable. Each room is furnished with two beds, and has a bathroom and a sitting room which opens out on to a small verandah, with a magnificent view of the beach and surrounding islands. There are taxis and trishaws to carry passengers from the ferry landing into town. There are no organized tours on Langkawi and getting around presents something of a problem. The main island does have 60 miles of motorable road and taxi drivers will hire out their vehicles by the day. It is possible to bring your own automobile by ferry, which, if you plan to stay several days, might be a good idea. There's much to explore around the island. One can travel

Country roads can be the most interesting. Photos by Robert Stedman

to most of the other islands by fishing boat.

The best time to visit is between November and April. The worst months are July to October during the southwest monsoon season, when it's wet and rainy.

There is ferry service from both Kuala Kedah and Kuala Perlis on the mainland. The ferry from Kuala Perlis is shorter and more popular. You can take your automobile, or leave it at the police station. Ferry departs at 1:00 PM daily. Fares are quite inexpensive and the trip takes about two and one half hours. During the holiday season there are other ferries in service but these are subject to change without notice.

In traveling in Southeast Asia, transportation is easily arranged. One option is to rent a car, which is simple enough to do. Every major car rental company promises the highest standards of safety, security and service at the best prices imaginable. Avis, for example, has a wide selection in its first class fleet of well maintained cars. A complete package comes with extensive insurance coverage and foolproof, backup service. Such service is only through major car rental companies.

You can also prearrange with a company to have a car waiting for you at the airport, with or without a chauffeur.

Two temples in southern Thailand. Photos by Robert Stedman

Unfortunately, at the present time, you cannot drive a rented car from one country to the next. Some car rental companies have fly-drive programs in which you drive one way and return by air. Thai Airways and Avis, for example, have a program by which you can rent an Avis car in Bangkok, take a drive through northern Thailand and leave the vehicle in Chiang Mai, or a number of other cities, and take a two-hour flight back to Bangkok. Thailand's Civil Aviation has allowed Avis to open six airport offices around Thailand. Or you can drive to Haad Yai, leave the car there, and fly to Penang and pick up another car there for your drive through Malaysia. Renting a car couldn't be easier.

Rental cars include 1000 cc to 2800 cc engines, and, if you feel that a jeep or a van will suit your plans, most agencies can arrange one for you. Rental rates dependent on your choice of a car and are cheaper by the week.

If you are worried about the driving rules in Southeast Asia, don't be. International driving rules and regulations are in effect and widely followed. Vehicles are driven on the left of the road. Generally, the speed limit is 80 kph (50 mph) in town and 100 kph (60 mph) on open roads. Three rules that I highly recommend are (1) stay in your lane, (2) don't make U-turns and (3) keep your speed down.

A driver must always be in possession of a valid driving license from his or her country of origin and the original or photocopy of the car registration book.

In Thailand, fines for traffic offenses are levied on the spot. If payment cannot be made, the driving license is retained by the police until the fine is paid at the local police station.

And as for that traffic problem you see in big cities, forget it. The problem is soon forgotten once you are on the open road. And just think, you can stop any place you want.

Chapter 7

MOUNTAIN CLIMBING
Scaling Southeast Asia's Highest Peaks

In no other place in the world can a mountain enthusiast find as much diversity as he or she can in Southeast Asia. The mountains here may not be as high as the Himalayas, but they do rival the Alps of Europe and the Southern Alps of New Zealand, except for the snow. Take Mount Tahan on the Malay Peninsula. It's not high, only 7,000 feet, but to reach its base before you even begin climbing, you have to hack through primeval jungles for several days, fording wild jungle rivers, and camping in a rain forest where elephants and tigers come down to the river to drink. And if it isn't wild beasts you have to contend with, it's leeches that can suck your body dry of blood.

And then there's Mount Kinabalu in the Sabah on the Island of Borneo. It reaches nearly 14,000 feet, higher than Mount Cook in New Zealand, and about the same height as the Matterhorn in Switzerland. To climb Mount Kinabalu, you start at sea level, not at five or six thousand feet as you do when climbing most other mountains. In comparison, it would be like scaling Mount Everest, but again without the ice and snow. Nevertheless, it can get mighty cold up there.

Mountain climbing in Southeast Asia has a challenge offered no where else in the world.

Beginning in Thailand and running down the Malay Peninsula, the land mass splits into two mountain ranges, with many mountains exceeding 2,000 meters, or 6,500 feet. Large areas of this high plateau were practically unknown to the outside world a hundred years ago. The blank areas on the map included most of the mountain peaks, most blanketed in clouds much of the time, and included one very mysterious mountain—Mount Tahan.

Mount Tahan literally means "forbidden mountain." For the orang asli who inhabit the jungle, the mountain is taboo. They believe its summit is guarded by a giant monkey.

The interior of the peninsula remained unexplored and unmapped until the end of the last century. Mount Tahan was seen and reported for the first time by outsiders in 1875.

Fifteen years later in 1890, H.N. Ridgley, Director of the Botanical Gardens in Singapore, made the first attempt to reach the summit. He never made it, not even part way, but his name did go down in history. He is the man I mentioned in the chapter on caves who took rubber tree saplings to Singapore and Malaya and tried to convince coffee planters to plant the young trees. He had little luck, until the pneumatic tire was invented and overnight rubber plantations appeared everywhere in Southeast Asia.

Other attempts to climb Mount Tahan followed. An Englishman named Belcher set out to reach the summit in 1883 but his attempt cost him his life. He was camped on a small island in the middle of a river when heavy rains upstream suddenly flooded the river. Belcher's camp was washed away and he was never seen again. Finally in 1905, H.C. Robinson, Curator of the State Museum in Selangor, succeeded, but it was no easy feat. The expedition had 65 people, two tons of supplies, including 55 bags of rice, and 14 dugouts to transport them up river. It took Robinson and his team almost three months to reach the summit.

Today, climbers can make it to the summit and back in ten days, or less if they are fit. I made two attempts before I succeeded. The first attempt ended in frustration, when I nearly froze and had to turn back. I quickly learned on that attempt that climbing any mountain peak in the tropics requires a great amount of preparation. Suitable camping gear, like tents and ground cloth, is needed, as well as clothing to protect from both rain and cold.

Climbers in the tropics have to pack in cold-weather gear, which might seem ridiculous. Aren't jungles supposed to be hot and steaming? Not so. Even during the day a tropical rain forest can be quite cold. Branches of trees above form a dense canopy of interlocking branches that screens out sunlight.

The ridges on Tahan are very broken, sometimes only a few feet wide, with sudden vertical drops of many hundreds of feet. The whole ridge line is covered in dense tangled vegetation and makes climbing extremely difficult.

Early attempts on the mountain failed because climbers approached from the most obvious route, up the Teku valley where it appears to be quite close. Once in the valley, the canyon walls along both sides have vertical walls almost three thousands feet high. Finally a dead end is reached by a series of spectacular waterfalls that tumble down 1,200 feet into the gorge.

The summit of Mount Tahan is often fogged in with clouds and mist. For the best effect, camp and spend the night on the summit to assure the cloud cover will vanish at some time or other and give you a spectacular view. Sunsets are beautiful.

Mount Trusmadi, 2,642 meters (8,669 feet), is the second highest mountain in Malaysia. The mountain is rarely visited, perhaps one expedition every year or two. It takes a number of river crossings to reach the base and requires a 30-mile hike to reach the summit. It's definitely not a tourist mountain. The final approach takes about eight hours, is quite steep and requires some rock climbing. Even more menacing than the steep climb are the pit vipers, poisonous green snakes that are well camouflaged. I have heard they only bite if stepped upon.

I have not climbed Trusmadi but I have been told by climbers who did reach the top that the actual summit is a small rounded area with low vegetation. Another mountain worth considering is Mount Murud. It stands at 2,423 meters (7, 946 feet) and is the highest mountain in Sarawak. It was first climbed in 1922.

Finally, there is the granddaddy of them all, at 4,101 meters (13,455 feet), Mount Kinabalu in Sabah on the north coast of Borneo, the highest mountain in Southeast Asia. It's a magnificent mountain to behold, and when you first see it, you can hardly take your eyes away from it. Lacking foothills, it shoots straight from flat low-lying jungle up into the sky, its jagged granite peaks floating above the clouds. When you

93

approach northern Borneo by sea, the mountain's summit becomes the prominent landmark. It is truly equally tantalizing and inevitably draws the attention of all travelers who see it. Even those who are not mountain climbers feel they would like to stand on its summit.

Up to about 3,000 years ago, the summit rock was covered with ice glaciers. There is no evidence that the summit of Kinabalu was ever actually climbed by local people in the distant past. In more recent times, local people were deterred by taboo and the cold. The summit was believed to be inhabited by the spirits of the dead, a very good reason for one wanting to keep well clear. Local hunters, barefoot and scantily dressed, and used to the moist lowland heat, could not travel in a rocky world where night temperatures plunge below the freezing point. Even early European explorers, equipped with thick clothing and blankets, found the summit tolerable for only short periods of time.

The first ascent of Kinabalu was recorded in 1851 by Hugh Low, a colonial official on the island of Labuan. The main problem was simply reaching the mountain. There was no road

Mount Kinabalu, the highest mountain in Southeast Asia, rises above the jungle of Sabah on the Island of Borneo. It's jagged summit appears like a controted dragon. The mountain is sacred to indigenous tribesmen.

or track running from the coast to the base of Kinabalu. One had to walk from village to village, taking on fresh guides and porters at each stage.

Climbers today can reach the base of the mountain on a paved road. It took Low fifteen days. He then hired local guides to take him and his party of 40 porters up to the highest known point ever reached on the mountain, Paka Cave, a big overhanging rock at 3,200 meters (10,000 feet), just below the present-day huts at Pannier Labia. After a needed day's rest, Low pushed on up the mountain and arrived at a point near present-day Sayat-Sayat huts and set up camp. A number of rock peaks soared up above Sayat-Sayat. Presumably thinking they were the top of the mountain, Low climbed up a gap between two of them just right of what is now called the Donkey's Ears. Rising clouds, which often envelope the peaks in late morning, forced Low to turn back.

Several years elapsed before Low made another attempt. This time he returned with Spencer St. John, the British Consul in Brunei, in April 1858. Unfortunately they had set off without proper climbing shoes and Low eventually had to give up

Left to right, Don Bianco, Joe Shafer and Harold Stephens, the author, at the summit of Mount Kinabalu. To reach the peak at 13,455 feet, climbers begin at sea level. It takes a grueling two days to reach the top.

again. St. John continued up the mountain without him. After three days his party scrambled up South Peak on the southern edge of the plateau. Seen from below, this conical peak of 9,989 feet, its sides smoothed by ancient glaciers, appeared to be the true mountain summit. Then the clouds swept up the mountain and the party was forced to retreat as mist obscured the route.

Three months later, in July 1858, Low and St. John returned to Kinabalu. They reached what they thought was the highest peak, set up the barometer that measured 4,097 meters (12,900 feet). They believed they had reached the summit, but they hadn't.

It wasn't until 30 years later that the highest peak, now called Low's Peak, was climbed. In 1888, John Whitehead led a major scientific expedition to Kinabalu. While on South Peak, he noticed a "large pile of loose rocks" to the north which appeared to be much higher. Scrambling up onto its top, he set up his barometer and discovered that this was the highest peak on the mountain.

Mount Kinabalu is the most popular mountain trek in Southeast Asia. To reach the summit from the base, and return, takes a full two days . The actual trail starts at the Power Station at 1,830 m (6,000 feet). It is then uphill all the way for about six miles to the 4,101 meter summit (13,455 feet).

The trail is well marked and maintained. To assist trekkers, ropes have been placed at the steep rocky section on the upper level. Trekkers from young children to people over 70 years old have followed this trail up to Low's Peak. No particular skill or experience is required; the route is suitable for the average person but they must be reasonably fit. The only essential equipment is a good pair of walking shoes or boots and a raincoat—plus some warm clothing, as the night temperature at mountain huts can fall to below freezing.

Care should be taken because not everyone, even those who think they are fit, can adjust to the high altitude. The air on the summit is only two thirds of the density at sea level, and you can quickly becomes breathless. Still, you won't know until you try. The key is to take it easy, as I learned.

For as long as I can remember, I wanted to climb Mount Kinabalu. But there was always one reason or another that I kept putting it off. I missed my first chance when I was writing a book on Malaysia for publisher Hans Hoefer. He and photographer Star Black climbed the mountain and Hans ended up writing that section of the book for me. When my next chance came, I didn't decline. Two friends from America, Don Bianco and Joe Shaffer, were touring Asia and wanted to do something different. We hit upon the idea of climbing the highest mountain in Southeast Asia. Joe is an avid climber, having scaled some of the highest peaks in both North and South America. Don had not climbed before but he has a home in the mountainous redwood country in northern California and is one of those people who is in great shape and doesn't know it. He proved it on Mount Kinabalu.

In spite of the great number of people who supposedly climb the mountain every year, you soon find yourself questioning your own ability. Judging by Mount Kinabalu's height at nearly 14,000 feet, that's like walking up the stairs to the top of the Empire State Building some 14 times in two days.

Furthermore, there's the weather to consider. It can get cold, and when you live in the tropics, a drop of ten degrees can be torture. Furthermore, before my climb, I met a European lady in Bangkok who told me her teenage son, who was fit and a member of his school's swimming team, had to abandon his attempt because of altitude sickness.

All this went through my mind when I tucked into my comfortable bed the night before my ascent. It wasn't that I lacked the experience, for I had climbed the Matterhorn in Switzerland and 18,000-foot Mont Popocatapetl in Mexico, but it's the anticipation before an event that is difficult to overcome. Once it begins, however, it's all different.

Times have certainly changed since Low's day on the mountain. We didn't need fifteen days to reach the base and another week to make the summit, and the route up the

97

mountain is nothing like it was then. Now it is a kind of celestial highway, with steps carved out of stone and open spaces fortified with planks, and in some places hand rails. It may make it all sound a little too easy but believe me, it isn't. When you begin climbing, you need all the help you can get.

We began our trek before dawn. The trail up the mountain is marked at 100-yard intervals, with notices YOU ARE HERE, but we found our progress was more easily judged by the shelters on route. There are six open shelters up to Panar Laban and a hut at Carson's Camp at the halfway mark.

The trail starts in oak forest. After a few minutes it dips down to a small waterfall, where we filled our water bottles. This is the only dip in the trail and from here on it was uphill all the way. Much of the area is secondary jungle—a forest that has been cleared and then abandoned. Such forest land is thick and tangled, and can be nasty for hiking. Fortunately, the track is well maintained and there is no need to deviate.

Among the most noticeable plants on this first part of the trail are the tree ferns and the pale pink flowers of the Kinabalu Balsam, a small plant found on the side of the trail.

We reached the first shelter, Pondok Kandis, at 1,981 meters (6,500 feet) in half an hour and were already panting. In another 30 minutes we reached the second shelter, Pondok Ubah, at 2,095 meters (6,900 feet). We had noticed many pitcher plants along the way, the small red and green living bowel-shaped plants that capture insects and devour them. Some they say even trap small wild animals and eat them.

Further up, flowering rhododendrons grew along the trail, hanging in loose folds from the branches of trees. Small ferns and tiny orchids grew on many of the trees.

At Pondok Low, the third shelter, my muscles began to ache. Markers told us we were at 2,286 meters (7,500 feet), only slightly less than half way. The trail now above the shelter steepened. Thick mist began to blow in, with an occasional light drizzle. With the rain, visibility dropped to zero.

Finally we reach Carson's Camp at 2,621 meters (8,600

feet), and broke for lunch. It took every effort for me to begin again, but once on the trail the beauty of the climb made me forget protesting muscles. There were more pitcher plants, now of a rare variety found only on Kinabalu, with the pitchers in beautiful shades of red and orange, with deeply serrated lips.

From Carson's Camp, we had two more shelters to go before we reached the summit, Pondok Villosa, at 2,942 meters (9,600 feet) and Pondok Paka at 3,052 meters (10,000 feet). At the last shelter there is a turnoff that leads down to Paka Cave, the large overhanging rock on the bank of a small, fast-flowing stream and the furthermost point on the mountain that the glaciers reached. This was the place to camp in the old days, before the huts were built.

After the last shelter, the vegetation quickly thinned out and the views became open vistas. It took another hour to reach Panar Laban where we spent the night at the modern Laban Rata Resthouse, a truly unexpected treat. Panar Laban marks the edge of the treeline at 3,300 meters (11,000 feet).

The view here at sunset was breathtaking. Massive layers of clouds were below us and the red glow of the setting sun gave the appearance that the world before us was on fire. In the distance to the south we could see jutting up above the clouds the jagged summit of Mount Trusmadi, the second highest mountain in Southeast Asia.

As beautiful as it was, our thoughts were not on sunsets and other mountains. We could only think about what was above us. We were aware that the trekking part was almost over and the climbing would begin in earnest. In the half light we could not see the rock face above us, but we knew it was there, and that the rope climb would begin.

It was indeed a restless night, at a time when rest was so needed. The wake-up call at 2:30 AM came all too quickly. We were told that it was necessary we begin at that ungodly hour to reach the summit at sunrise.

After we started, I was convinced there was another reason for the early start. If it were daylight, one could see the threatening rock face above, and few people would venture beyond the resthouse.

But in the darkness all you see is the light of the flashlight the person in front of you is carrying. The climb now was almost sheer, and so exhausting we had to stop to rest every few minutes. Don went ahead with his guide, to be certain to have his camera set up on the summit to capture the sunrise.

The guides had told us that it would take about three hours from the resthouse to reach the summit. They didn't say you had to have Sherpa blood to do it. It took Joe and me an hour just to reach Sayat hut at 11,400 feet. The hut marked the end of the vegetation. From here on out, it was bare rock.

Above and behind the hut the rock goes almost straight up to two jagged pinnacles. The route leads to the west and runs parallel with these pinnacles. To help climbers at this point, rangers have strung rope over the rock face to give people something to hang on to and help pull themselves up. It's impossible to see the top, only the dangling rope before you. Joe and I, and the other climbers in our group, took hold of the ropes and began our ascent. The rounded shape of South Peak began to come into view, just as dawn was breaking.

South Peak is at the southern edge of the summit. When you reach the plateau, a wide area of flat, smooth rock appears. I could see the chatter marks made deep in the granite by a million and a half years of glacier flow. It is a half-mile walk across this plateau before Low's Peak comes into view.

It was much lighter now and we feared that the sun would break over the horizon before we reached the summit. It was a 500-yard walk across the plateau, the path marked with cairns of rocks, when Low's Peak came into view. I remembered now about our guide telling us how two climbers got lost on this very same section and were never seen again, despite a team of professional mountaineers from America searching for them for several weeks.

Each step now was an effort and our lungs ached terribly. Don and his guide were no where in sight, and we couldn't help wondering if they might suffer the same fate as the two men our guide mentioned.

We finally reached the last pinnacle, Low's Peak, just as the sun was breaking the horizon. We looked up, and in a bright red glare appeared the summit, 100 yards above us, and there, sitting on the very top of the world, was Don and his guide. Joe and I closed the final distance just as the sun broke above the horizon, like a fireball being hurled at us by some mighty, unseen force.

That view from the summit, at sunrise, is spectacular. In the distance we could see the Trusmadi Range. To our west was a clear view of the coastline and the South China Sea. To the north, close by, there stood St. Andrew's Peak and Victoria Peak. And on our eastern side, the summit dropped straight down, almost vertically into Low's Gully.

The summit of Mount Kinabalu is covered with thin plates of rock, much like fish scales, but larger. Geologists tell us that Kinabalu was born only one and a half million yeas ago when it was formed by a mass of molten granite, under very high pressure deep in the Earth, which then forced its way upwards. Now at the surface, the pressure is being released causing the rock to come off in flakes.

We were instructed that we had to leave the summit before 10:30 AM. After that, clouds race up the mountain and immerse the summit in mist by early afternoon. If this happened, we could be trapped for the night in freezing weather.

We signed the log book kept in a nook in the rocks at the summit, and I was surprised to find how few signatures there were in the book. Of the many thousands who profess to make the summit, how many really make it? Or are they too tired to sign in?

Elated, we now began our descent. By evening we reached the base at Park Headquarters, so weary and muscle sore, we had a difficult time getting up from the dinner table once we sat down. But we had made it. We had reached the summit of the highest mountain in Southeast Asia.

For those who might consider climbing Mount Kinabalu, there are a few pointers to remember. Bring plenty of warm clothing, adequate rain gear, walking shoes, a torch, a water bottle, a hat and a pair of gloves. Energy-giving food such as chocolate, nuts, raisins and glucose sweets are good during the ascent. Sleeping bags can be rented at the Laban Rata Resthouse. Visitors must utilize the services of an authorized guide for the ascent to the summit. Porters may also be hired. Guides and porters are not employees of the Park, and the Park only undertakes to put visitors in touch with them.

The key to a successful climb is to take your time. Do not allow other people to make you rush. If you become tired, then stop and rest. Young people often rush up Kinabalu. They then develop altitude sickness and have to turn back. In contrast, older and wiser people go up slowly resting when short of breath, and eventually arrive. To reach the huts at Panar Laban or Syat Syat on the first day, set off early the next morning and reach the summit around dawn. After taking photographs, you begin the descent. You can easily be off the mountain before dark.

For those daring souls who are interested in rock climbing, the Kinabalu massif does offer some fine opportunities for the sport. But one doesn't have to travel to Borneo to find interesting rocks to climb. One of the best and most challenging area is the cliffs at Railey Bay near Krabi in southern Thailand. At Railey Bay they call it sport climbing, which means the routes up the limestone cliffs are marked by permanent bolts set two to three yards apart. Climbing is done in pairs with one person belaying—feeding the rope—to the second person who climbs.

There are more than 200 climbs around Krabi ranging from beginner to advanced levels, all within a short distance of each other. Those who have climbed before can hire equipment, buy a route book and go it alone, or they can hire a guide. For beginners, a number of climbing schools offer courses ranging from half-day tasters to a three-day series.

Chapter 8

YACHTING COMES TO SOUTHEAST ASIA
Junk Cruising to Yacht Chartering

My Chinese friends in Singapore were very proud of me when I announced I was building a yacht at a shipyard in Jurong. They always suspected that I might be a rich tokay, masquerading as a poor writer, and now it was confirmed. They looked forward to the Onassis-type yacht I would build, and the day that I would invite them aboard for cocktails. Their first disillusionment came when they learned I was going to build it myself, with my own hands. This doesn't set well among Asians, where a man with an education is not expected to do so much as hang a picture on a wall without calling a handyman in to do it. Then when I began driving around town in an old Chinese truck, they politely disassociated themselves from me. The complete end of our friendship came when they saw my schooner launched and anchored in front of the clock tower in the Singapore Harbor. It was a sailing boat, and not a shiny luxury yacht. It had masts, and not twin diesel powered engines with turbo chargers. And imagine ratlines going up the rigging, with a jutting bowsprit, just like the junks in olden days that sailed into Singapore. My fiends wanted to see a super yacht, not a replica of a vessel that brought their ancestors out of China, a type of sailing craft they were trying to forget. No, I had lost face with all my Chinese friends.

That was a while back, more than twenty years ago, and times have changed. Yachting, after a long struggle, is finally coming of age in Southeast Asia. More and more cruising yachts from abroad are finding new pleasures in Asian waters, and Asians themselves are discovering that sailing can be as much fun at home as it is in the Mediterranean, and certainly much cheaper. Take a look at Phuket on Thailand's Andaman Sea. When I sailed my schooner into Patong Bay in 1976, I had the whole bay to myself, aside from local fishing boats. Now there are annual yacht races that originate in Phuket, and bring yachtsmen from the world over, and there are now the world-famous King's Cup Race in the Gulf of Thailand.

Tourism to Southeast Asia has done much to bring about the sudden awareness of what Asia really has to offer, other than temples, massage parlors and good shopping. The sea is one. Those things that once frightened would-be sailors away—mainly pirates and typhoons—are no longer the obstacles they once were. As one intrepid visiting yachtsman said. "Pirates! You find more in Florida and Hawaii."

As for storms, we learn that typhoons exist in belts which can be avoided. Hong Kong and the northern Philippines are in that belt and are unsafe during the typhoon season, approximately four months out of the year. The area below that is free of typhoons and includes the southern Philippines, all of Borneo, Singapore, Indonesia, Malaysia and Thailand. That's a lot of cruising ground. Early seafarers called this area "the land below the wind."

Same for monsoons. When the Northeast Monsoons blow, it's time to sail to the west coasts of Malaysia and Thailand, and all the way to Phuket in southern Thailand. In April or May,

The author's schooner Third Sea anchored at a small cove off Ko Samui on the Gulf of Thailand, waiting for the monsoon winds to change.

when the Southwest Monsoons move in, the wise captain moves to the east coasts and perhaps up to Pattaya and Bangkok, or he sails to Hong Kong and the Philippines. It's all a matter of the studying charts, and the seasons.

The big advantage of yachting in Asian waters is if you want to change your environment, or culture, the distances you have to travel isn't that great. Where else can you find half a dozen cultures within a radius of a thousand miles?

Other than blue water and sandy beaches, there are some added attractions to yachting in Southeast Asia that you don't find in the Pacific, the Mediterranean or the Caribbean.

First, let's consider islands in the sun. Even the phrase, islands in the sun, rings with romance. It would take several lifetimes to visit even a small portion of the tropical isles with pristine beaches in Southeast Asia. Philippine charts list some 7,100 islands while Indonesia has a chain of islands, more than 13,000, that stretch some three thousand miles from one end to the other. Yachting in the Philippines, however, is confined only to the north, due to the political uncertainties in the south, and in Indonesia, due to sailing permits and government

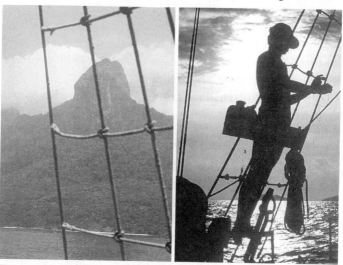

Tioman Island, off the east coast of Malaysia, was a landmark for navigators for thousands of years. Yachtsman on right checks the rigging before dark.

regulations, pleasure sailing in these waters is restricted and not recommended. There are exceptions, of course, and that is if you sail direct to Jakarta or Bali and don't make stops in between.

Thailand, Malaysia and Singapore, on the other hand, are dotted with islands on both their coasts, and even tiny Singapore has 52 islands. Yachting in the waters of all these countries is safe.

The beauty of some of these storybook islands is legendary. When MGM needed an idyllic isle to film James Michener's imaginary Bali Hai for the musical South Pacific, they chose Tioman on the East Coast of Malaysia.

Tioman, 140 miles from Singapore, is beautiful. It has two excellent bays with safe anchorage, and a most interesting jungle path across the mountain that connects the two. Several other beautiful islands neighbor Tioman. Rawa has a white sand beach and a resort where yachtsmen stop for cold beer. Tinggi has the shape of a perfect cone.

Farther to the north of Tioman along the Malay coast are two more islands that capture the hearts of dreamers. They are Perhentian and Redang. My favorite is Redang. It appears like a picture postcard. The water in the bays — there are two — is so clear you can see your anchor on the white sand bottom 40 feet below. At one of the bays is a Malay fishing village, unchanged since time's beginning.

In the Gulf of Thailand farther to the north is Ko Samui, known these days to most travelers. It has some excellent coves with good anchoring. North of Ko Samui are two smaller islands, Ko Phangan and Ko Tao. Thais here live in scattered villages. When I first sailed there in my schooner some twenty-five years ago, I reported that there were no roads, only trails connecting the villages. No hotels, no electricity, no shops, no food stalls. That has pretty much changed. But what hasn't changed is the coral reefs around Ko Tao. They are alive with sea life.

The West Coast of Malaysia and Thailand are ideal during

the Northeast Monsoon. Pangkor is popular. Penang is Singapore fifty years ago. Yachtsmen can anchor right downtown in front of the clock tower in old Georgetown, not overnight but long enough to pick up supplies and discharge and pick up passengers and crew.

The Langkawi Islands lie 60 miles north of Penang on the Thai border. They number 99, and like the fjords of Norway they create an exciting labyrinth of waterways and passages. Sheer granite cliffs drop abruptly into the sea, their walls worn white and serrated by weather and the passage of time. One island, uninhabited, has a freshwater lake with a white crocodile, more legend than real, while still another has a waterfall that cascades down the granite rocks to form seven pools. Each one of the smaller islands can be a paradise in itself, without facilities.

A day's sail north of the Langkawi Islands, or three days if you make island stops at night, is Phuket Island, Thailand's most popular island resort. For the yachtsman, Phuket is an island surrounded by a hundred smaller islands, each one more magnificent than the last one.

At the southern tip of Phuket is Ko Racha Yai, a small sun-drenched island where, when you anchor, the water is so translucent your yacht appears to be floating in space. Farther to the east are the Phi Phi islands, the most beautiful of all the Phuket isles. So powerful is the sight of them as you approach, they are certain to leave impressions so deep they remain etched in your memory forever.

Sheer limestone cliffs rear up like contorted dragons, forming Phi Phi Don, the larger of the two islands. Phi Phi Lay, the smaller of the two, lingers in the background. At uninhabited Phi Phi Lay, take your dinghy and explore Viking Caves. So called because of curious, inexplicable ancient paintings of Nordic-looking boats on the wall. Could the Vikings have come this far a thousand years ago? Swim into tiny grottos and caves where the dappled light creates endless pictures.

In another cave you can marvel at frail wooden scaffolding where energetic Thais scale the flimsy structure to gather birds' nests for making the famous Chinese soup. Trade in this commodity has been going on for thousands of years, a trade built not on gold, or silver, or precious stones, but birds' saliva.

Ko Rak Nok, a delightful little rock of an island, has a waterfall 780 feet high and a beach of phallic carvings where Thai fishermen come to give alms in hope their barren wives can give birth.

Next, consider the rivers of Southeast Asia for cruising. It's a pity but most yachtsmen avoid rivers, yet they can offer some remarkable cruising waters. One of the great rivers of Asia is the Chao Phraya, the River of Kings that flows down the very center of Thailand and empties into the Gulf of Thailand. Time was when a yachtsman could sail up the Chao Phraya and anchor in front of the Oriental Hotel, as Joseph Conrad once did with his bark *Otega*. I was fortunate to have done the same with my schooner *Third Sea*, but that was a year or two before they built the Sathorn Bridge down river from the Oriental Hotel. Sitting on deck in the evening, with the Oriental Hotel to our starboard and the sun setting over

Sailing schooners were once a familiar sight on the Chao Phraya River, but the construction of the Sathorn Bridge below the Oriental Hotel brought an end to high-masted sailing ships on the river. Seen here are Royal Barges.

Thonburi on our port, was like living in a world of fantasy. But it was real, and like all good things, it had to end. The construction of the Sathorn Bridge saw to that. Nevertheless, one can still sail up the River of Kings for nearly eighteen miles and anchor or tie up to docks and wharves at Klong Toey below Bangkok. Yachts that can lower their mast can sail all the way to Ayutthaya, the ancient capital of Siam that was sacked by the Burmese more than 200 years ago. Cruise boats make the journey every day. The Chao Phraya is a great river for yachtsmen, but few ever take advantage of what it has to offer.

There are dozens of other rivers that will accommodate deep draft yachts, even the tiny Malacca River. I took my 70-foot schooner up the narrow river to Malacca (impossible, old salts told me) and tied up where Dutch and Portuguese ships moored 400 years ago.

In Borneo it's an easy sail up river to Kuching, but the real thrill is the Rejang River into central Borneo. It's navigable all the way to Kapit, the last outpost. An Englishman named James Brooke did it in his schooner a hundred and some years ago. I followed in the wake of Captain Brooke, except that I didn't have cannons aboard. He did, and drove out the pirates,

Sailing ships, some a hundred or more feet long, make their way to the barter trading port on the Pandang River in Singapore. Occasionally sailing junks loaded with charcoal also make their way down the Malacca Strait from Burma.

Sailing the waters of Southeast Asia is different than sailing the South Pacific. Distances are not so great. Yachtsmen can change cultures from one day to the next. And tropical storms, except for northern Philippines, are nonexistent.

and so pleased the sultan that he was made the White Raja of Sarawak, a status he and his heirs held until after World War II when the country became independent.

Not actually a river, but close to it is the Klang Estuary, a maze of waterways, where the jungle reaches to the water's edge, that leads to Port Klang. Countless small islands, some too tiny to name, make up the estuary. None seem more than a dozen feet above water. Casuarinas and scrub brush blanket the land down to the water's edge where mud flats and mangroves begin. There's one island above the others that I like to visit. It's called Ketam. It's a fishing settlement, with 16,000 Chinese inhabitants, 90 per cent of whom are engaged in fishing. The settlement, constructed entirely of wood, is built high above water on stilts, and when you walk the planked streets, you have little idea that the sea is below.

In the roads near Port Klang great steamers, freighters and tour ships drop anchor, all with exciting and mysterious names. *Jaladharrna* from India, *Orchard Garden,* Singapore, *Hana Maru*, Japan. And the luxury cruise ship, *Island Princess*, churns slowly through the waters en route to Penang and Sumatra.

Then there's history. To sail the seas of Southeast Asia is to sail through history. China was trading with India when Rome was still on outpost on Greek maps. Both Tioman in Malaysia and Phuket in Thailand were part of the Indian-Chinese trade route. Excavations on Phuket have produced Greek and Roman earthenware, golden Arabic coins, and Chinese pottery. And on Ko Phi Phi there are wall murals in the caves that I mentioned, murals said to have been left by the Vikings.

Tioman Island which lays thirty-five miles off Malaysia's East Coast, is an unopened history text book. On the southern end are twin peaks called Ass's Ears, a landmark for seamen for 2,000 years. A thousand years before the arrival of Europeans, Chinese merchants made Tioman a port-of-call. Ming pottery has been discovered in caves in the hills, and one recent visitor reported finding a gold chain of uncertain Chinese origin in a stream bed in one of the rivers.

On Malaysia's west coast in the Strait of Malacca is the old pirate hangout, Pangkor Island. It has an old Dutch fort, and history that has yet to be written. The island has some fine coves to anchor. And to the south of Pangkor is Malacca, one of the oldest European settlements in Asia. It was visited in 1410 by Chinese Admiral Cheng Ho, the Three Jeweled Eunuch, captured and settled by the Portuguese, sacked and claimed by the Dutch, traded with the British for Bencoolen on Sumatra, and granted independence by the British to the Malays in the 1960s. What more history could any yachtsman ask for?

Finally, yachting offers diving for both fun and profit. Perhaps you are interested in diving for lobster and looking at pretty coral formations, or diving on a thousand-year old Chinese wreck and a World War II battleship near by. In Southeast Asia waters both are possible. I discussed these possibilities in detail in Chapter 3, "Treasures Beneath the Sea."

Yachtsmen are forever arguing where are the finest waters for diving–Phuket, Tioman, Palawan. These are all excellent, and no one wins an argument as to which is best. It becomes a personal matter, like red wine or white wine.

There's no denying, yachting in Asian waters has a romance all it's own. What excitement, sailing through the Conradesque world of Southeast Asia. Consider the Dindings and the Klang Estuary that I mentioned. You drop anchor in front of a village, and in the evening when the harsh noonday glare of sunlight is reduced to softness, you become subtly aware of a skyline silhouetted by the onion domes and minarets of Muslim mosques. And when you have your evening meal on deck under the awning, with the sun setting in a blaze of oranges and reds behind the village, you can't help but feel Asia to the very tips of your fingers. It's the combination of many things–smells that come from the village, from copra and coffee plantations, and that of sounds, the imans, Muslim priests, calling out evening prayers from the tops of their minaret towers. You feel then that the world, your private world at least, is at peace.

What my Chinese friends in Singapore thought to be a horror story is what is happening right now in the waters of the Andaman Sea around southern Thailand. Junk cruises! First class "junk cruises" are being offered these days at Phuket. But in all fairness, the junks here are not like the ones that came down from China in the salt trade half a century ago. *Suwan Machais* is an example. She's a restored junk, with a powerful diesel engine that provides not only power to propel her forward when the wind fails, but also the energy for refrigeration, electric lights, radios and ship-to-shore communications, things the Chinese immigrants, my Chinese friend's ancestors, never dreamed possible. These junk cruises are first class affairs, sponsored by Thai Airways International's Royal Orchid Holidays.

If you really want to sail in first class splendor, go aboard the four-masted clipper ship *Star Flyer*, also operated by Royal Orchid Holidays. This is really a superb sailing vessel that cruises the Andaman Islands around Phuket and sails all the way down the Malacca Strait to Singapore. It's certainly reminiscent of days gone by when square riggers ruled the seas, except those vessels of old didn't have swimming pools and cocktail bars aboard, as the proud *Star Flyer* does.

Something else has taken place and become the latest craze since I first sailed my schooner many years ago into Patong Bay on Phuket–a new water sport called sea canoe adventures. There is a purpose behind the madness of going to sea in a canoe. The madness is that there are some very lovely spots you can only reach by canoe. The waters around Phangnga Bay have some of Southeast Asia's most spectacular scenery. Limestone outcroppings rise up from the bay's calm waters, thrusting skyward a hundred yards or more into the air. Within many of these monoliths are deep caves that open into still lagoons of magnificent beauty. Open to the sky, they hold mangrove forests, many of them inhabited by families of monkeys that have been stranded there eons ago when the ice age melted and the seas rose. That's where sea canoes have an advantage over most other water craft. You can reach these once inaccessible grottos and hidden lagoons with these rugged two-man inflatable sea canoes.

That is yachting today in Southeast Asia. It's a sport that's growing fast, with government regulations easing up for both boat owners and visiting yachtsmen. More and more foreign yachts are appearing on the horizon each passing day, and scores of yacht clubs are springing up everywhere you turn. What will this new millennium bring?

Chapter 9

BIKING SOUTHEAST ASIA
Mountain Biking on Elephant Trails

Biking is an ideal way to discover Southeast Asia's diverse cultural and natural heritage. Bikers, both novices and veterans, will find challenges here they never anticipated. Imagine, cycling through centuries-old architectural ruins, and have stone figures of gods and goddess staring down at you as you pass. Or where else, except northern Thailand, can you pedal through hilltribe villages that even four-wheel drive vehicles cannot reach, and where you have to give way to elephants on the track to get there. Where else can you find such exotic touches? Mountainous terrain one day, with brooding scallop-shaped limestone formations, like prehistoric dinosaurs, all about you, and the next, beaches that line the coast, beaches worthy of the best Mediterranean resorts.

Granted, cycling is not the fastest way to get around, but bicycle rides on small country roads do give you complete freedom from bus and train schedules. From a bicycle, you enjoy unsurpassed closeness to nature and meet people outside the circuit of mass tourism.

Cycling is not new to Southeast Asia. After all, local people have been getting around on bikes ever since the two-wheel vehicle was introduced more than a hundred years ago. And let us not forget, the Japanese captured Singapore not by engaging in a naval battle as the British expected they would, but instead by coming down the Malay Peninsula on bicycles through the back door. But what is new is cycling vacations for foreign visitors, and in a sense, the awareness of biking for pleasure for many Asians as well.

A decade or two ago, two expat business men in Bangkok decided to cycle from the Thai capital down the Malay Peninsula to Singapore. They made the trip in three weeks, and also made headlines. It was something no one had ever done, or even considered. Today when motorists see long-distance cyclists on the roads and highways of Southeast Asia, they think nothing about it. Nor do Asians consider it odd any more when friends, and even their own children, set off for distant points, even other countries, on bicycles.

Cycling in Asia, much like yachting, has come full circle. It's spreading rapidly to every country in the region, and bike tours are being offered by both local and international tour operators. Even Thai International's prestigious Royal Orchid Holidays offer bike tours as an option for planning a vacation in Thailand.

Some counties in Southeast Asia are, of course, better geared for biking than others. Thailand, Malaysia and Singapore offer the best opportunities for those who want to enjoy a biking holiday. Other countries are less certain. Although I would not hesitate to rent a bike and cycle around Rangoon or Mandalay, I would think twice about cycling outside these cities into the country unless it was on an organized tour authorized by the government. The same might apply to certain towns, cities and resort areas in Indonesia, Laos and Cambodia.

Again, there are some exceptions. I mentioned briefly in the chapter "Digging into Southeast Asia's Past" about renting a bicycle in Siem Reap in Cambodia and cycling to Angkor Wat. Years ago it was possible. It was a delightful ride to Angkor, along a quiet road, in the shade of great eucalyptus trees, with the sound of birds and insects filling the morning air. My arrival at the gates of Angkor was always one of sheer joy, no matter how many times I had been there. I would spend the day, and the days after that, cycling among temples half eaten by the jungle, eating my packed lunch on a crumbling temple wall. My most cherished memories of Angkor Wat go back to 1966 when I traveled with a group of journalists, accompanying Jacqueline Kennedy Onassis on her visit to the temples. She was awed by Angkor Wat.

I recently returned to Angkor Wat, and this time watched tourists being rushed about in air-conditioned buses. I realized at that moment how much more enjoyable a place can be when your pace is slow and leisurely, as one surely experiences when riding a bicycle. Travel restrictions in Cambodia at the present time prohibit bike trips to the ruins but hopefully this policy will change. Cycling within the capital city in Cambodia is possible, however.

Bikers in Southeast Asia are constantly looking for new areas to explore. The most recent discovery is Vietnam, made by a group of American war veterans, middle-aged ex-soldiers on sentimental journeys to the past. They found Vietnam to be much better the second time around than the first, and safer. Their bike tour took place in the summer of 1999. Most remarkable about the tour was that it was made up of disabled American veterans, some double amputees. They were joined by Vietnamese war veterans from both the north and south, and they cycled *en masse* northward from Saigon, or Ho Chi Minh City as it's called today, to Hanoi. They wore bicycle shoes instead of combat boots, and bicycle shorts instead of camouflage fatigues. Featherweight bicycle helmets replaced the metal clunkers that protected them 30 years ago.

Bicycles parked on a main street in Shanghai. China has more bikes per capita than any other country in Asia. Photo by Robert Stedman

117

The goal for most bikers is to cycle from Hanoi to Ho Chi Minh City. It's a 1,200 miles, two-week biking trip that follows legendary Highway One, built by the French, bombed by the Americans, and is still the country's two-lane backbone.

The biggest obstacle along Highway One today is not snipers but potholes. Unlike land mines, potholes can be dealt with. In one place, the highway climbs 3,000 feet in a devilish six miles, with 210 switchbacks and only 25 feet of flats, or so it seems. The highway settles down and opens up, with sweeping views of the South China Sea, paving the way through a marvelous landscape.

The principal downside to bicycle touring in Southeast Asia is the general condition of most larger roads, or trunk roads as they are called. These major roads are generally crowded with trucks and speeding buses, plagued with pollution, and often lack any sort of bike path or even a shoulder to follow. Fortunately, many of the newly constructed highways do provide marked areas for cyclists.

On the positive side, smaller roads are rarely used by commercial vehicles and are generally deserted except for a few motorcyclists and private cars. Some very popular cycling routes are those found in northern Thailand, starting from Chiang Mai and branching out in every direction. Bicyclists can put their bikes on top of buses and head off to a remote location before tackling the back roads. Bicycles can be transported on almost every form of transport, from minivans to tour buses, and even flown around the country on Thai Airways. And more commonly now, you can rent a bike.

In Malaysia, following the coastal roads makes for easy riding and you have two coast lines to choose from. Back roads along these routes pass through small kampongs, or villages, and wind their way through vast copra and palm oil plantations. Also along both coasts are some interesting islands to explore. Bikers can easily pack their bikes aboard ferries.

Rides through the northern hills of Thailand can be scenic but also exhausting. There are no cutaways; the road system follows every rise and fall of the topography. A more pleasant option are the country roads that skirt the Mekong River, such as the winding stretch from Mae Sai to Chiang Saen and Chiang Khong. When you've reached the limits of your endurance, you can flag down a bus and throw the bike on the roof for the remaining distance to the next town.

Bicyclists will also enjoy the flatter rides from Sukhothai in central Thailand to the nearby historic sites of Si Satchanalai and Kamphang Phet. There are some fine Khmer ruins, much like Angkor Wat, in this area. Another fine scenic route leads from Nong Khai to Chiang Khan, in northeastern Thailand. This quiet little strip of asphalt is relatively flat, offers splendid views over the Mekong River, and is dotted at convenient intervals with small towns that have inexpensive overnight accommodations.

Don't rule out biking around Chiang Mai. The road from Doi Inthanon National Park to Mae Chaem Valley and Op Luang Gorge is one of the most picturesque and most challenging, with a series of sharp plunges and steep climbs.

The 15-mile Doi Inthanon-Mae Chaem section is strictly for experienced bikers with its downhill slopes and sharp turns. The trip may take anywhere from one to three hours. The 20-mile Mae Chaem-Op Luang route is a succession of straight roads punctuated by steep ascents. The first half of the route is under the jurisdiction of the Forest Industry Organization, which manages huts for overnight camping. The second half is easier, and this trip should suit bikers of intermediate skills.

Exploring hilltribe villages north of Chiang Mai requires the use of mountain bikes, and is often combined with four-wheel drives on the Mae Suai- Ban Huai Krai-Doi route.

One of the finest and most thrilling biking areas is around Mae Hong Son. Nestling between mountains and valleys and shrouded by mist for most of the year, Mae Hong Son is home to many highland tribes and immigrants from the Shan State of Myanmar, or what used to be called Burma. Pai District is the ideal starting point for biking explorations of the hilltribe villages, waterfalls and hot springs in the area.

Ayutthaya is the old capital of Siam, which was sacked by the Burmese 200 years ago, and is a major attraction for those who like historical grandeur. And what better way is there to see the sites than by bicycle. Fortunately, there is little traffic on the roads into town, so biking around the ancient city is quite safe. Most of the sights on the historic City Island are a good bike ride apart. One of the most popular routes is the Bang Pa-In Summer Palace. A great way to get to Ayutthaya from Bangkok is to load your bike aboard a ferry and take a cruise up the Chao Phraya to the capital. Most river hotels in Bangkok have their own boats and run river excursions.

When it comes to getting advice on biking in Southeast Asia, I turn to an old friend, Mick Elmore. Mick is a biking enthusiast who began his Asian experience as a copy writer for the *Bangkok Post* in 1992. Two years later he turned to free-lance writing. He is a stringer for several wire services including the highly respected German agency, Deutsche Presse-Agentur. Mick keeps an apartment in Bangkok and gets around on a bike. When he travels around the region, which is often, he takes along his bike. He has biked through Japan and across Southeast Asia as far as Australia. I don't know anyone who has traveled Asian byways more than Mick.

Aside from Bangkok, Mick lived for a year in Phnom Phen, and found the Cambodia capital a great place for biking. Vientiane, the capital of Laos, was equally pleasant, with very little traffic.

Mick has some sound ideas about cycling. "Bicycling is the most efficient form of transport, bar none," he explains. "You travel further for energy expended than any other way, including walking, riding horseback or driving. It's true the driver uses less energy when he drives a car than when he pedals a bicycle, but when you consider the energy used by the car, it is actually a very inefficient mode of transport."

"The environmental aspect of pedaling is appealing. You

are exposed to the elements. Perhaps it may be a pain at times, but you get a genuine feeling for a place when you travel by bike. And biking doesn't harm nature, unless, of course, you tear through fragile terrain on a mountain bike, digging into the soil, and breaking plants at the base."

Mick believes mountain bikes should only be allowed in given areas and riders should not be able to travel at will through open forest areas unless along marked trails and roadways. I asked Mick about breakdowns.

"Bicycle repair is always a worry when making a long trip," he said. "But learning the basics, such as fixing flats, adjusting cables and chains and replacing spokes is always wise. This is particularly important if you plan to travel to remote areas."

Mick pointed out you usually don't have to go very far to find bicycle repair shops when you get into difficulties. In most Southeast Asia countries, motorcycle repair shops can fix most problems for a small fee.

Like many other cyclists, Mick's favorite biking country is Thailand, especially the north. He is a frequent visitor to Chiang Mai, but rather than spending a week to cycle the 500 miles, he puts his bike on a train in Bangkok and makes the trip overnight, or else rents a bike when he gets there.

Mick suggests biking from Chiang Mai to Mae Hong Song by way of Pai. "You can do the whole circuit in a week," Mick said. "In Pai, ask the locals about some of the good side roads to take. There's lots of ups and downs in mountainous terrain, and the road can get narrow."

The northwest is safe for bikers but Mick does take precautions. "Once you get off the main roads, it's all dirt road, and much more interesting," he explained. "But you do have to be careful about ending up in Burma. That happened to me once. I ended up in Burma and didn't know it until Burmese soldiers stopped me. I didn't even see a border marker. I was fortunate. The soldiers motioned for me to go back the way I came."

Another great trip that Mick suggests, which isn't as mountainous as the Mae Hong Son trip, is one to Chiang Rai. From there bikers can do a loop through the Golden Triangle. There are pleasant, inexpensive hotels and it's possible to cycle along the Mekong River for long distances. The ride to Mae Sai reaches the northernmost point in Thailand.

As I mentioned, south of Chiang Mai is the highest mountain in Thailand. Mick believes if bikers are fit they can ride their bikes from Chiang Mai, make it to the summit, and be back by nightfall. He also agrees that the road from Doi Inthanon National Park to Mae Chaem Valley and Op Luang Gorge is one of the most picturesque routes in the north, and the most challenging, with a series of sharp plunges and steep climbs. He warns that the 15-mile Doi Inthanon-Mae Chaem section is strictly for experienced bikers due to downhill slopes and sharp turns.

Mick's first time, he had a heavy, steel-frame Taiwanese bike and it took him nine hours to cover the 30 miles from the border of the park to the summit. The route up the mountain is not very well engineered and is almost straight up, or so it seems. The view from the summit is breathtaking.

"On the way down, it took 90 minutes," Mick said. "You can wear out your brakes and have to be careful. This is one place in Southeast Asia where you can ride a bicycle to the highest point in the country."

Mick finds that the northeast, called Issan, is not as dramatic as the Chiang Mai area, but it is still quite interesting as it is the cultural center of the country. One drawback is you can't get off the main road and find adventure on dirt roads as you can around Chiang Mai. "You pretty much have to stick to main roads," Mick said. "They are main roads, but you really ride through history. I can't think of a better way to see the Khmer temples at Phimai than by bike."

Mick has some good advice for those planning a biking trip. Try to be on the road by eight in the morning. Aim for 60 miles a day or less. You can reach your goal by early afternoon and have the rest of the day for leisure. It's not advisable to ride in the heat of the afternoon. In any event, you do want to reach your destination before dark.

You don't need much to bike the roads and byways of Southeast Asia. It's not necessary that you wear a helmet on back roads, but a good sun hat is a must. Gloves and glasses are essential, and wear shoes that you can also walk in. In the winter months, December and January, take along a sweater. It's not advisable to camp at night in the tropics, and, besides, it's not necessary. Accommodations are plentiful and inexpensive.

Mick contends that you don't need a high-priced mountain bike with a CAAD 2 frame to enjoy biking in Southeast Asia. Road conditions are acceptable for street bikes. Also, bicycles can be rented for very little by the day or week. Rental shops and guesthouses with bikes for hire are located in nearly every town frequented by Western tourists. Some visitors purchase bikes and then resell them prior to their departure.

Mick Elmore in Singapore, preparing to set off for Thailand, a 700 mile journey, with an electric bicycle he was testing for a local manufacturer, Singapore Technologies. He can travel 30 miles or more per charge.

Ardent cyclists should consider bringing along their own bikes. Airlines often have lenient policies about accepting bicycles as luggage, especially bikes that can be disassembled and carried in a bag. Bicycles brought from abroad should conform to accepted international specifications to simplify the replacement of wheels, spokes, and gear systems. Avoid delicate racing bikes with skinny tires and be sure to take along a comprehensive tool kit, pump, and heavy-duty steel cable lock for security.

The last time I saw Mick was in Singapore, as I was preparing this text for the printer. The day was gloomy, with dark menacing rainclouds overhead. It was the height of the monsoon season. But Mick was in bright mood and no rain cloud was about to dampen his spirits. He was on his way from Singapore to Thailand, via the west coast of Malaysia, by bicycle. But this was no ordinary bicycle. He was testing an electric bike for Singapore Technologies, a company that introduced for the first time electric bicycle in Singapore the year before.

Manufactured in Shanghai, the electric bike can travel up to 20 miles (32 kilometers) per charge, with a full recharge taking six to eight hours. The Singapore Government has authorized the production and sale of the electric bicycle for they see the electric bicycle as an environment-friendly form of commuting. And at 10 US cents per recharging, it's also inexpensive. "It's a great bicycle for the city," Mick said as he adjusted his glasses and made ready to depart.

"But you're not driving in cities," I said. "You're touring, and Thailand is 700 miles from here."

"We'll see," he said, and I watched him head toward the Causeway that leads to Malaysia.

Chapter 10

ARCHEOLOGICAL DIGS
Rewriting History

I remember Professor Carroll Quigley of Georgetown University's School of Foreign Service lecturing students in his "Development of Civilization" class, and telling us that two things are needed before a society can become a civilization—writing and city life.

For decades Dr. Quigley, like most other historians at the time, had placed the cradle of civilization in the Middle East. The development of writing, the very first cities, the wheel, the first use of bronze—they all began, he contended, around 3500 BC in Mesopotamia, in what he called the "Fertile Crescent," the valley between the Tigris and Euphrates Rivers that flow through modern Iraq down to the Persian Gulf.

Historians would have thought no different had pieces of broken pottery not been found in northern Thailand. History was about to be rewritten. The frenzy began when a young American named Stephen Young, a Harvard sociology student and son of a former American ambassador to Thailand, stumbled on a prehistoric burial site near the village of Ban Chiang and noticed the shards of pottery. He showed his find to the Fine Arts Department in Bangkok, and history was turned topsy-turvy.

For nearly a century, residents of the Ban Chiang area had encountered pots, beads and even human bones when digging around their houses, but they had paid little attention to the finds, not realizing how important they were. Now with Steve Young's discovery, the Fine Arts Department decided to investigate the matter, and excavations at Ban Chiang began. The year was 1966.

The Fine Arts Department submitted fragments of round-topped pots for carbon testing, and discovered they dated back to around 4600 BC. More excavations unearthed a rich collection of iron and bronze tools and utensils, buried alongside human skeletons. The discoveries would prove to be more important than anyone had even expected. Before long Ban Chiang would be making headlines around the world and become a household name in academic circles.

Could these discoveries mean the dawn of civilization began not in the Middle East as history recorded it, but instead in a small village in a remote corner of northern Thailand? Serious excavations were now needed. From the University of Pennsylvania came American archeologist, Dr. Chester Gorman, and assigned to the project from the National Museum in Bangkok was the Thai archeologist, Dr. Pisit Charoenwongsa.

Gorman and Charoenwongsa began digging in earnest at the Ban Chiang site, and were soon uncovering bronze artifacts in ancient grave mounds in both Ban Chiang and nearby Non Nok Tha, along with some pottery dating from between about 4600 and 3500 BC. Within two years, they unearthed 126 human skeletons and 18 tons of artifacts. The pair identified seven separate layers of remains at Ban Chiang. The lowest, reaching back to about 3600 BC, was some 16 feet (5 meters) below ground level; and it was

Fake pottery, exact duplicates of original pieces, are being produced today in Bang Chiang village.

here that the diggers found their historical bombshell not only a bronze spearhead lying beside a skeleton but also a second skeleton that was wearing bronze anklets and a third with bronze bracelets.

Specimens of their finds were sent to the University of Pennsylvania for Thermo-Luminescence testing, and the results were far beyond what anyone had expected. They were older than Mesopotamian bronzes from 3000 BC and Chinese bronzes from 2000 BC. They predated by at least a century the nascent cultures of European civilization.

The excavations gave proof that prehistoric man settled in this part of northeastern Thailand between 3600 BC and 200 AD. By around 2000 BC, they had mastered bronze and later iron manufacture, and then developed skills in making pottery and glass beads, in weaving techniques and in the cultivation of rice.

As a result, the consensus among historians about Europe being the cradle of civilization had been challenged by this seeming insignificant discovery—bronze artifacts, found thousands of miles east of Mesopotamia around the other side of the world.

An obscure little village in Thailand was suddenly catapulted into worldwide fame, and was lauded as the founder not only of the Bronze Age but of the Iron Age as well. Up until 40 years ago, archaeologists considered Southeast Asia a cultural backwater—they thought its arts and civilization to have been borrowed from India, China and even Europe. Bronze technology, it was believed, only arrived here from the Middle East around 500 BC. The implications of the Ban Chiang find are staggering since they may eventually lead archeologists to make a wholesale revision of early human history in both the Far East and the West.

Other sites in Thailand have also yielded pottery of a similar age (4600 to 3500 BC) to that at Ban Chiang, adding more unanswered questions to an already long list. Meanwhile, the hunt goes on for more evidence to piece together the full story of the history of mankind, and the answers may be right here in Southeast Asia.

Chet Gorman certainly believed so. I was fortunate to have befriended him in the late 1970s, and traveled with him when he went to meet Dr. Dato Shahrum, the curator of the National Museum in Kuala Lumpur. Chet had hoped that he could continue his digs in the north of the Malay Peninsula and possibly get government support. He was convinced that jungle area of both northern Malaysia and southern Thailand might prove to be just as interesting, and rewarding, as Ban Chiang had been. He was quite disappointed when he learned that the Malays, for the most part, are xenophobic and don't want outsiders coming from abroad to do their archaeological work for them. To the contrary, Chet was quite concerned about the invasion of archaeological sites in Southeast Asia by anyone, both locals and foreigners. He was especially disturbed about the artifacts that were being stolen from Ban Chiang before the government stepped in and Ban Chiang was declared a World Heritage Site.

Chet was an incredibly curious man. He was interested in most everything, but his appearance was hardly that of Indiana Jones. Bearded, with reddish hair, he was heavy set and charged about in battered jeans and white sneakers. He was deeply interested in sailing, and before entering college he had hitchhiked around the world. He was fascinated with Australia and the islands of the South Pacific.

He was very articulate. Conversation with him was invigorating. He had studied math and physics in college, and was interested in energy fields. He went into paleontology which he combined with geology and archaeology. He admitted he was, at first, interested in space. He had married young, and moved with his wife and infant son to Hawaii to complete his undergraduate work. But Chet's wife, not taking to the academic life, left for the States. They divorced some years later.

Chet Gorman's career with the University of Pennsylvania

was well established, but fate would play its hand and Chet never lived to see his dreams fulfilled. When working under a fierce sun and in a downpour of tropical heat, he developed a small blister on his back. He didn't think much about it, even after it began festering. When he discovered it was cancer, it was too late. At the age of 43, he died at his family's farm near Sacramento in California. His son was at his side.

Chet believed that more research is needed in the study of the prehistory of Southeast Asia, and that the area is still very much a blank page. He believed that if the research were done, Thais will find themselves the proud possessors of a civilization predating even those of China, India and Egypt.

Ban Chiang may seem a long way to go to see skeletons, but for those who have an interest in history—not only of Thailand, but of mankind—it's well worth the effort. A good start is a visit to the Ban Chiang Museum, one of Thailand's finest show places. Unfortunately, shortly after Ban Chiang became known as the new 'cradle of civilization,' large-scale looting took place at the site and, sadly, few intact pots were retained for the museum.

Aside from the Ban Chiang archaeological site, it is believed that much pottery, ceramics and metal artifacts, as well as skeletons and other items, remain to be discovered. Many are certain that historical evidence and archaeological traces are scattered throughout the entire area, far more than what is on display at the museum or the excavation site.

Dusting old bones isn't everyone's idea of excitement, but one can hardly turn a cold shoulder when they see Khmer temples half buried in a tropical rain forest. In the chapter on 'Lost Cities' I mentioned the discovery of Angkor Wat in Cambodia by the French naturalist Henri Mouhot, but I didn't mention that Angkor Wat is only one of many hundreds of similar Khmer ruins scattered throughout Southeast Asia. It's highly likely that there are some still to be discovered.

Consider Thailand's vast northeast, an area covering 56,000 square miles, or roughly one-third of the country. It's the poorest and least-developed part of the country, a dry and arid plateau which hardly receives enough rain to produce one crop of rice each year. Yet poor in agriculture, it's rich in history. The old Mon-Khmer kingdom once flourished in these parts, and today it's famous for its fine Khmer-style temples, such as those we see at Phimai. But this is only a very small part of what was once the mighty Khmer Empire. There's Laos, Vietnam and Cambodia.

Between the 10th and 14th centuries AD, a large part of mainland Southeast Asia from the Mekong Delta in the east to the Chao Phraya River in the west lay under the control of the Khmer Empire. Administered, at the height of its power, by god-kings like Surayavarman II, their capital was at Angkor, connected to its outposts by a network of military highways that, in a way, resembled Rome and its famous Apian Way. These outposts were grand cities in their own right — Phimai, Preah Vihear, Wat Phu and Phanom Rung.

By the mid-19th century, these grand Khmer cities were lost, even to the memory of man. The Khmer Empire had long since disappeared by the time French imperialists carved

This photo of Angkor was taken by the author in 1966. Soon after, the ancient ruin was closed to the world. It was recently reopened.

130

the lands into separate states and created Indochina. The one exception is Thailand who remained independent.

Visitors today only have limited access to Angkor Wat but Thailand's doors are wide open. The Thais have long valued these historic treasures, and realize their importance as tourist attractions. Over the past three decades several of the most important sites have been painstakingly and successfully restored by the Department of Fine Arts. The Tourism Authority of Thailand is able to promote a "Khmer Culture Route" in lower Issan which offers visitors an unparalleled opportunity to explore the glories of the great Khmer past.

An ideal way to see the ruins is to rent a car and do the driving at your own pace. The westernmost, and best-known of these sites, is Phimai, 37 miles northeast of Khorat. In the distant past, the site was directly linked by road to Angkor, the capital of the Khmer Empire. Phimai was the main religious and administrative center of the Khmer northwest.

The complex at Phimai dates originally from the reign of Surayavarman II, during the first part of the 12th century,

A view of Anchor Wat as it looked in 1966 before Cambodia entered a civil war. The author, right, made yearly pilgrimages through the ruin by bicycle.

131

and was dedicated to the cult of Vishnu. The central sanctuary tower and much of the immediate surroundings which survive today date from this early period. About 100 years later, when Jayavarman VII, "the builder," extended and developed Phimai, the temple became a Mahayana Buddhist center, dedicated to the Vimaya Buddha.

Phimai may be the best-known, and the most easily accessible Khmer ruin in northeast Thailand, but Phanom Rung to the south is perhaps better preserved, and certainly set amidst more spectacular scenery. The temple complex is a rather confusing mix of Thai and Khmer. It was originally built as a Hindu temple honoring the deities Vishnu and Shiva. The sanctuary rises from the crest of an extinct volcanic cone 4,900 feet above sea level, offering fine views of the surrounding countryside.

It's interesting to note that between 1961 and 1965, a stone lintel had been illegally removed, and investigations showed that it had been donated by James Alsdorf, an American benefactor, to the Oriental Art Institute in Chicago. After a long and vigorous campaign by the Thai people, the lintel was returned to Phanom Rung in 1988.

Phanom Rung in southeast Thailand reflects a past glory of the great Khmer Empire that once ruled the region. Photo by Robert Stedman.

About 50 miles south of Phanom Rung stands a temple that is rarely visited, and much less well-known than nearby Phanom Rung. It's the old Khmer sanctuary of Prasat Muang Tam, and dates to the late 10th century AD.

Other gems in the "Khmer Culture Route" may be found in the provinces of Surin and Sisaket. Two noteworthy ones are Prasat Sikhoraphum and Ban Pluang, the later of which dates from the second half of the 11th century and was once an important stop on the road between Angkor and Phimai. A third temple complex farther on and well into Sisaket Province is the sanctuary of Prasat Kamphaeng Yai. Hopefully, in years to come, when peace returns fully to Cambodia, Preah Vihear (known to the Thais as Khao Phra Viharn), and just across the Cambodian border from Thailand, will open to the outside world. In the summer of 1998, I attempted to enter the ruin with photographer Robert Stedman but we were stopped short by Cambodian soldiers. We returned to Bangkok to read in the *Bangkok Post* that several foreigners were captured and held prisoner shortly after we left the area.

Geologists tell us that Thailand apparently served as a land bridge between Asia and Australia through which

A tumbled mass of masonry at Wat Phu in southern Laos. Beheaded stone statues at Borobudur in central Java. Photos by Robert Stedman.

133

successive racial groups filtered down from China and Tibet. These Proto-Malays encountered the Pleistocene and Hoabinhian-era inhabitants, who were forced south or absorbed by the new arrivals. Few of these peoples survive aside from isolated highland tribal groups such as the Malaysian Dayak, Sakai and Negrito.

Prior to the arrival of the present inhabitants, Southeast Asia was home to several Pleistocene cultures (600,000-130,000 BC) who left behind stone implements, pebble tools, and other artifacts from Lampang in the north to Krabi in the south. Later period Hoabinhian (120,000-3000 BC) tools and farming implements have been discovered near Mae Hong Son and Kanchanaburi and all the way down the Malay Peninsula to Borneo.

The Kanchanaburi findings were uncovered by Chet Gorman in 1972, when he discovered tools and seeds in Spirit Cave near Soppong in Mae Hong Son Province. His findings were carbon-dated back to 10,000 BC, and pottery and polished knives from 6000-6800 BC.

The land bridge from Asia to Australia was marked with endless caves and deep caverns. These caves offered natural protection for early man. It was in such caves in northern Borneo that my first interest in these dark secrets of Southeast Asia began. They were the famous Niah Caves of Sarawak.

Although the Niah Caves were known as far back as the 1870s—when an animal collector noted their existence—it wasn't until the 1950s that they made world headlines. A curator from Sarawak Museum thought they might have some archaeological potential and began excavating. Sure enough, when he dug down five meters he found the skull of a young *Homo sapiens* who had lived in the caves 40,000 years ago. It is the earliest known remains of modern man in this part of the world. As the museum delicately probed the layers of soft deposit, it unearthed the evolution of a human culture. Many agreed it was the greatest discovery since the Java Man.

Being hunters and food gatherers, early man did not spend

all his time living in caves. He moved in the area around his cave and went there not only for shelter and protection but also to bury his dead, to perform religious and mystical ceremonies and to decorate these sanctuaries as holy places. Cave walls which have been preserved under hundreds of feet of guano are time capsules waiting to be opened one day to reveal our past. Some remarkable and mysterious cave drawings dating from the dawn of early man have been found.

Steve Van Beek, the author of *The Arts of Thailand,* an excellent documentation of the history of Thai art, stated that we can safely say the caves of Thailand are the country's first museums of modern art. "On limestone walls," he wrote, "Stone Age artists drew ochre and black stick figures as well as full-bodied humans and animals cavorting in empty space. In these primitive landscapes, birds, tortoises, frogs and herds of cattle appear at random, often overlapping one another without regard to the others' right of prior domain. Perhaps the artists drew in light so dim they could not discern the outlines of figures previously sketched there."

Some of these murals, like the ones found in the Viking Caves on a small island near Phuket, have baffled archaeologists and travellers ever since they were discovered. Blanketing a length of wall about 30 feet long and six-to-eight feet high, the drawings—painted with different shades of clay—show a disjointed fleet of ships.

Size and design vary from junks with pleated sails to galleons sporting row of oars. Some appear on the verge of collision or battle, others sail alone in shadowed corners.

Some believe they might be a vivid portrait of what might have been pirate practices in the past. Others concluded that there is nothing esoteric about them at all. It so happened that the many caves is this area contain one of the world's most expensive and rare delicacies, swifts' nests, used for making Birds' Nest Soup. The islanders say the gathering of bird nests has been going on for hundreds of years. This may be a key to the mysterious cave drawings. Could not the drawings have been made by dutiful nest protectors, bored with the endless months of cave living, and their wall dabblings are nothing more than graffiti?

Another story that can trigger the imagination is that the drawings were left by alien visitors. It all depends upon what you want to believe.

Other such paintings on the walls of a limestone cave on Koh Khian Island in Phang-nga Bay, a short distance from Viking Caves, are thought to date from prehistoric times. They are devoted to figures of animals and abstract patterns.

Much of our human past is cloaked in mystery and remains unknown. For hundreds of centuries our ancestors left no written records; for many more centuries they recorded events haphazardly, if at all.

Clues to our past keep turning up everywhere. The sudden finding of long-buried artifacts in a cave on Tioman island off the coast of Malaysia can indicate an ancient trade route. The discovery of shards in a field plowed by a Thai farmer in the northeast might prove an ancient culture once survived on the same spot. Modern scholars are constantly broadening our historical horizons by means of increasingly sophisticated archeological methods and technological advances. But when it comes down to the final analysis, it is the Stephen Youngs of the world who do the ground work and make remarkable discoveries by simply being curious. Indeed, there's more to Southeast Asia than crowded cities and good shopping.

Chapter 11

GREAT AND NOT SO GREAT TRAIN JOURNEYS
From Orient Express to Jungles of Borneo

For train buffs, there's no shortage of train journeys in Asia, everything from coal burning chuggers to sophisticated modern expresses. Each one is an experience in its own right. Travelers, however, usually have fixed ideas about train travel in the East. Generally, what comes to mind when you mention train journeys in Asia—the Orient Express!

Few names can conjure up more romance than the mention of the 'Orient Express.' Intriguing plots for spy stories, novels and movies, all have been built around this legendary train trip from Europe to Asia.

There is only one problem: the name is a misnomer. It's true, there was once a transcontinental Orient Express, and it did start in Europe, but it terminated where Asia merely began, at the gates of Istanbul. Although an Europe-Asia line may have been a great dream of rail magnates from time to time, there never has been a through train from Europe to the Far East, say from London to Singapore. The gaps in the route are too many—eastern Iran, Afghanistan, Burma, nor does such a dream look hopeful in the near future. In fact, 50 years ago it was easier to travel a greater part of the distance by rail than it is today.

But rail buffs travelling in Asia need not fret; there are some great train trips that would be hard to equal in the West. You hear talk and see advertisements about the E&O Orient Express, but this line, which is quite new, doesn't connect Asia to Europe. It runs from Bangkok down the Malay Peninsula to Singapore, but more about it later.

Perhaps the closest thing to the old Orient Express is the Trans-Siberian railway, from Moscow across Siberia to the Sea of Japan, a 2,500-mile journey.

The famed railway was started in 1890 and completed just before the 1917 Revolution. Closed to foreigners down through the years, it was only opened to general travel about twenty years ago. No sooner had Intourist, the official Soviet Government tourist bureau, announced its opening, than I applied. Regretfully, I can't say I made the Trans-Siberian journey. Intourist granted my visa for an overland journey, but it was to drive. I covered a 5,000 miles in Russia in an old army jeep I bought for the occasion. But I still look forward to the rail trip one day.

Those who have travelled on the Trans-Siberian line call it an experience of a lifetime. By boarding the train in Moscow, passengers cross the entire expanse of Siberia to Khabarovsk in the Russian Far East. From there it's an overnight train ride to the port of Narodka, near Vladlvostok, aboard a special tourist train. Then it's a 48-hour ocean voyage to Yokohama.

The only complaint about the Trans-Sib, as seasoned travellers call it, is that the seven days it takes can become awfully boring. And the window blinds in the compartments are kept closed most of the time.

"Now, take the Bullet Train in Japan," diehard train buffs will tell you. "It does 200 miles per hour."

What these people don't tell you about the Japan ride is that you have to book days, and sometimes weeks, in advance, and if you don't you are certain to spend a thousand miles, or five hours, squeezed into a compartment that required several ex-sumo wrestlers at the doors to pack everyone in.

Nor for great train rides can I recommend Indian trains. Your chance for getting first-class tickets are better than in Japan, except that you might find in your compartment half a dozen other passengers holding first-class tickets too. But even worse, unless you close and lock the doors, when the trains starts to move, an army of people without any tickets at all will try to rush aboard. Since Indian trains have no passageways connecting compartments, no conductor will come to assist you.

Every Asian country, with the exception of Afghanistan and Laos, has at least one railway in operation, some offering exceptional rides. In the island Republic of Indonesia, for example, there's a very popular line, and air-conditioned, which operates a daily service between Jakarta and Surabaya. I have taken it a couple times on my way to Bali. The only negative thing about the trip is that it's overnight, and there's not much you can see in the dark.

If you happen to be in Savannakhet in Laos, and go to the railway station there, don't expect to buy a ticket. There's no railway, only a station. The French, it seems, built the station but never got around to constructing the rail line.

Nevertheless, there are some exciting rail journeys. Most train travel in Asia, however, is within individual countries, with one exception, an international service from Bangkok down through Malaysia to Singapore. It's a two and a half day journey that runs the entire length of the Malay Peninsula.

Perhaps the fact that there is a train running the length of the Peninsula is intriguing enough to tempt one to try it. The building of the rail line can be compared to the digging of the Panama Canal. Engineers on both sides had to fight nature and battle a myriad of diseases and fever before they could succeed.

The design for the railway station in Kuala Lumpur, left, was rejected; it could not hold two feet of snow as required by law. Vendors at a stop in Thailand.

Prior to the railway, towns of Malaya were only pockets of civilization, each one existing in isolation. Even Kuala Lumpur, the capital, was little more than a jungle village hidden away amid dense forest. The only means of commuting was by way of a narrow jungle track, on an elephant's back or by bullock cart. At most, one could only cover ten to fifteen miles a day.

In most opinions of the time, construction of a rail line — the cutting of a path through a seemingly impenetrable jungle — was an impossible task. But it was more than clearing a jungle; there were vast gorges and rivers to be bridged and swamps to be crossed. Surveyors discovered in some areas they would have to descend through eighty feet of mud before they could reach solid footing,

The jungle provided other obstacles that were even more formidable. While labor crews battled intense heat and disease, they also had to fight off beasts of prey that continually plagued them. One report states that seldom a day passed without a hungry tiger snatching up a lone worker and dragging him into the jungle for his evening meal. Even after the rail line was completed, the threat of the jungle continued. There's one rather tragic example.

Shortly after the section between Tapah Road and Telek Anson was completed, a passenger train met with an unprecedented accident. While defending his herd, a wild bull elephant charged the train head on and derailed it. No one was hurt but the impact did throw the engineer from his cab into the jungle. The track was blocked for five days. The head and tusks of the elephant are on display in the National Museum in Kuala Lumpur.

The railway station in Kuala Lumpur was constructed long before the first track was ever laid. When Sir Frank Swetenham submitted the design for approval to the head office in London, it was rejected. The roof, they said, couldn't withhold two feet of snow as was required in Britain.

The first rail line in Malaya was opened on June 1, 1885,

connecting Port Weld with Taiping, covering a distance of eight and a half miles. Eighteen month later another line was opened, connecting Kuala Lumpur to the coast. The line made headlines. It was no less important than our modern day landing on the moon.

The Straits Times, dated September 22, 1886, called it a momentous occasion, with brass and royalty aboard, from His Excellency the Governor and Lady Weld to His Highness the Sultan of Selangor and his hundred attendants. "It started at twenty to ten and at quarter past eleven the train steamed into Kuala Lumpur, the run of about twenty miles having been done in ninety minutes."

The article goes on to say that "when the train neared KL the speed was greatly accelerated and we were doing about thirty miles an hour." The article concluded by saying "the motion was very pleasant."

What did the arrival of the Iron Horse mean? One reporter saw it as a tourist promotion scheme and nothing more. In the same paper he wrote: "The train will mean an increase in foreigners and strangers who will come, much to the profit of the country."

Singapore island had its own rail system but it wasn't until 1923 that the causeway connecting the island with the Malay mainland was completed and carried the first through train from Singapore to Penang.

As I mentioned, the newest train in Southeast Asia today is the E&O Orient Express, which travels from Bangkok to Singapore and back again. Two other trains also make the run to Singapore, one an international express, the other through the highlands of central Malaysia.

The E&O Orient Express has been in service only a few years. It's the talk of Asia today, with its first-class, quality service. The special service is an attempt to recapture the old Orient Express of yesteryear. So far, however, there have been no murders to live up to it's namesake. Nevertheless, it has "coat-and-tie dining" on gourmet meals and luxury private compartments, with hot showers and room service. The cost for the three-day trip doesn't come cheap.

On the other hand, the old International Express has been around for decades. The price of a second-class, air-conditioned sleeper, from Bangkok to Singapore, is a mere fraction of the cost of the E&O, but, as one might think with such a price discrepancy, the International Express must really be a cattle-car train. It isn't. In fact, it's a very pleasant and comfortable train trip.

Every time I tell people I am traveling to Singapore by train on the International Express, they think I must be crazy. "You can fly for just a little more," they insist. That's true, but they miss the point completely.

So what is the point? What's the attraction about riding the rails in Southeast Asia?

The International Express is a touch of the old days. Travel by jet, has but one purpose—to get travelers from A to B. That's it! We have forgotten that the real fun of travel can be the "getting there."

A year had passed since I took the International Express

The Penang ferry, for both cars and passengers, a sixteen-minute ride from Butterworth on the mainland to Georgetown, the capital of Penang.

142

to Singapore, and I was curious to see if there had been any changes. I bought a ticket at Hualamphong Station in Bangkok—one way, second class, air-conditioned sleeper, Bangkok to Penang—for one thousand baht, less than thirty US dollars.

I chose to stop in Penang for two reasons: it makes a nice break in the journey to Singapore, and Penang is a great town to visit. In Penang, I planned to buy another ticket on the day express to Singapore.

This wasn't my first train journey aboard the International Express. My first time was 1960, and since then I've made the trip at least once, sometimes twice a year. In the old days it was even more often, at least from Bangkok to Penang. I wrote for the *Bangkok World* newspaper then, and we had to renew our visa every three months. We could either take the night train to Penang or travel by bus to Vientiane in Laos. Most of us chose Penang.

I was surprised by the changes at Hualamphong Station. Signs were now in both Thai and English. A row of neat kiosks selling everything from newspapers to snacks lined

Haulamphong Railway Station in Bangkok. After an incoming train failed to stop and crashed through the building, the station was rebuilt.

one side of the station, and behind the kiosks were food stalls and a restaurant.

A few years back the station had to be rebuilt, and not by choice. An incoming train traveling at high speed failed to stop and came crashing through the station, almost out the other side into the taxi stands. The station not a new face-lift.

The launching of the new E&O Orient Express must have had something to do with the changes too. Conductors now stand in front of their cars ready to assist passengers. Not like before. They wear white shirts with epaulettes, and caps with golden emblems of the State Railway of Thailand. They are polite and smiling, and will pose for a picture.

Those who call the International Express the 'cattle run' should come aboard. Cars are new, or nearly new, stainless steel and spotlessly clean. They are divided into compartments, each with seating for two, facing each other. At night the compartments are transformed into upper and lower berths. Attendants in uniforms, like airline hostesses, come through the cars handing out plastic bags for trash. Before passengers just threw their rubbish on the floor or else out the windows.

My only complaint is that I enjoyed traveling much more in non-air-conditioned cars. The price has nothing to do with it! It was pleasant to travel with windows open. I liked to look out of an open window; I liked to feel, to smell, to breath in the countryside; to let the wind blow in my face; and when we reach a station and the train came to a halt, I liked to listen to sounds—the mulling, the shouts of the people, the conductor's whistle, the chants of vendors. From the vendors, carrying heavy-laden trays and baskets upon their heads, I liked to buy all those delights the Thais have to offer—barbecued chicken with red sauce, sticky rice in bamboo with mango, baked fresh corn in its husk, sweets neatly wrapped in woven green leaves, tropical fruit and so much more.

Today, all the cars are air-conditioned, with the exception of third class. You can still find a few vendors on the platforms selling their wares, but now you have to step off the train to buy from them. It's not quite the same.

The International Express train departs exactly at four o'clock in the afternoon and makes a grand sweep through Bangkok before turning south towards the Gulf of Thailand. The train rumbles across a bridge over the mighty Chao Phraya River and the city gives way to industrial sites and finally open farm lands, mostly rice fields.

They call it the International Express but the stops are frequent, every half hour or so. My second disappointment, other than open windows, is that there are no longer dining cars. Hostesses take orders for dinner and breakfast and deliver the meals to your seat. Both Western and Thai food is offered on the menus. No more sitting up half the night in a dining car drinking Singha beer or 'Mekong and soda' with train guards and policemen. I don't even know if they have the guards any more. Train robberies aboard the express were once common, but robbers these days find the tourist business more profitable.

Relaxation is the key to train travel. It's your chance to read, gaze out the window, or just nap. The tune of click-idy-clack as the train rumbles down the track is bewitching. But, if you are like me, you can't nap very long. There's too much to see. I can't take my attention away from looking out the window, watching the countryside flash by. It's a lazy mood, a much needed mood in our modern day of constant rushing.

The conductor begins to make up the sleeping berths around eight o'clock. I sat up and watched a magnificent flaming red sun set. We were in an area where limestone outcroppings rise up high from a flat plain and they look more like skyscrapers than the works of nature they are. The setting sun plays hide-and-seek behind the mounds and then disappears. I waited but it didn't reappear; only the reddened sky remained. It was time to turn in.

I had a lower berth; I undressed and pulled the curtains closed, again conscious of the sound, click-idy-clack, click-idy-clack. The motion of the train was surprisingly smooth, like the *Straits Times* reporter had said a hundred years ago, and sleeping is enjoyable.

It was a beautiful morning, and I felt rested after a great night's sleep. I had breakfast at my seat. Rice fields in every shade of green appeared. No more water buffalo. Farmers now tend their fields with two-wheel tractors that look like push carts.

Trains no longer permit smoking on-board, which really must be hard on the Chinese. I remember cars filled with smoke, and the Chinese coughing at night, and especially in the morning. Chinese are noisy. They have to scream and shout, and they let their kids run wild. Two Cantonese gentlemen sat in the next compartment, across from each other, and they spoke so loudly it sounded like they were fighting, but it was only a friendly conversation in their harsh southern Chinese dialect. Mandarin Chinese, the dialect of the north, is not like this. In fact, it's rather pleasant sounding. But few Chinese in Southeast Asia speak Mandarin.

I wandered around the train. I walked through the third class compartment. It was non-air-conditioned; the windows were open. There were a few foreigners, backpackers, blocking the isles with their huge, overweight packs. They slept curled up on their reclining seats. The overhead ceiling fans buzzed wildly.

It was ten in the morning when we arrived at the Thai-Malaysian border, where we had to go through customs and immigration. Passengers must take their luggage and belongings with them and proceed to customs. The Malay immigration officers couldn't be nicer, even when they told me it is forbidden to take photos, after I had already snapped half a dozen shots.

At noon we arrived at Butterworth, the terminal across a narrow strait from Georgetown, the capital of Penang. After a pleasant night on the island, I left the next morning at eight by train for Singapore. I arrived that night at ten.

There is a second southern route to Singapore that few

people know about. A little more complicated, but interesting, it's a branch line from Haat Yai to Sungai Golok on the east coast. Although this is the end of the Thai line, passengers can cross the border and continue by rail from Kota Bahru in Malaysia to Singapore. The crossing is not difficult. From the railway station it's only a short distance by trishaw to the Thai immigration post on the border. Here porters are on hand to take you to the Malaysian immigration and customs. From here, taxis make the 18-mile run through some lovely Malay country side into Kota Bahru, for a small fare. From Kota Bahru the rail line that runs down the central highlands of the Malay Peninsula to Singapore. It is an exciting train trip through some dense jungle, where tigers and wild elephants still dwell.

Thailand has an excellent rail network. Prior to the advent of the railway, less than a hundred years ago, animal-drawn vehicles had been virtually the only means for land transportation in the Kingdom of Siam. At the time, the population was sparse and the country far less modernized. By the turn of the century, if you wanted to go to Chiang Mai in the north, you needed three weeks to a month to make the 500-mile trip. The 160 miles from Bangkok to Pak Nam Pho took one day by train, and from there to the next town upriver it was six days by boat, followed by 11 days over caravan trails via Lampang to Chiang Mai.

It was King Chulalongkorn, Rama V, the monarch responsible for abolishing slavery and establishing public schools, who introduced the "iron horse" to Thailand. On his trips abroad, both to Asia and Europe, he had come to know and appreciate railways. He envisioned a Thai rail network as a way to unite his country and provide a means for economic development. A railway would be the most efficient way to reach his subjects in remote regions, as well as those areas rich in teak, tin, rubber and rice.

In March 1891, he passed a Royal Proclamation authorizing the construction of the first railway line in Siam, leading from Bangkok to Korat (Nakhorn Ratchasima). Six years later, on March 26,1897, the first 40-mile track from Bangkok to Ayutthaya was completed and opened to traffic.

The railway system greatly expanded throughout the country under the reigns of Rama V and his successor Rama Vl, when most of the present rail network was completed. Today the State Railway of Thailand (SRT), offers passenger and freight services to all regions of the country.

In the early days, steam engines ruled supreme until 1928, when two diesel locomotives were imported from Switzerland. The end of the use of steam was in sight. However, even today a few wood-burning, steam engines are still in use, although not in a revenue-earning service. Many railwaymen and train buffs were sorry to see these old beautifully maintained engines go.

Since the 1880's, it had been the dream of railwaymen to build an international line from Singapore up the Malay Peninsula through Thailand and Burma to the Indian subcontinent and to Europe. The plan became a partial reality when the Japanese built a line from Thailand into Burma, but at a great cost—some 16,000 Allied prisoners of war and more than 100,000 Asians. It was the notorious "Death Railway," a feat that was accomplished in just one year between October 1942 and October 1943. The line fell into ruin after heavy bombing by the Allied forces and today is little more than a tourist site.

Thailand has four main trunk lines plus a few minor side routes, totaling 3,000 miles (4,500 kilometers). They handle over a 100 million passengers a year and more than six million tons of cargo. Of the passenger traffic, 97 percent use third class, while only three percent go first and second class, most of them foreigners.

The main lines include the southern route to Hat Yai, where the line splits, one fork going to Sungai Golok on the east coast and the other branch entering Malaysia at Padang Besar. The northern line ends in Chiang Mai. The northeastern route runs to Korat, where it forks into the lines ending at Nong Khai and Ubon Ratchathani. The eastern line goes to Aranya Phrathet and continues into Cambodia.

The second most popular train route in Thailand is the northern run to Chiang Mai, located in the hills some 500 miles north of Bangkok. The overnight express leaves Hualamphong Railway Station at six each evening and arrives in Chiang Mai at 7:40 AM the next day. The so-called Rapid Train leaves Bangkok daily at 3:45 PM and arrives in Chiang Mai at 6:35 the next morning.

There was a time, not so long ago, when passengers on the Chiang Mai Express had to close their compartment windows between Bang Mun Nak and Taphan Hin. It seems that when the train stopped in Bang Mun Nak, monkeys would swoop down from the trees and climb on top of the compartment roofs. They rode the train to the next stop at Taphan Hin, where they jumped off into the trees only to catch the next train back to Bang Mun Nak. Nobody would have minded them sneaking a free passage, except that they were stealthy little devils, and when the passengers were asleep, they helped themselves to whatever they could carry off. They were mostly after food, but wrist watches and cameras were sometimes carried off, too.

Service on board the express trains is good, and there are sleepers on both lines. The linen is clean and you can even take a shower if you wish. Compartments are air-conditioned, and thus closed to monkeys.

A line which is seeing more service is the northeastern line to Nong Khai, the Thai border town on the Mekong River, 390 miles (626 kilometers) from Bangkok and 13 miles (21 kilometers) from Vientiane, the capital of Laos. The overnight express leaves Bangkok's Hualamphong Station at 8:30 every evening. If you want to see something of the countryside, you may prefer the morning train that arrives in Nong Khai in the early evening the same day.

In November each year, this northeastern line is fully

booked, at least to Surin, for the annual elephant roundup that takes place there. Trains leave Bangkok one day and return the next. It is a popular trip and one of the best recommended train journeys in Thailand.

An interesting line that's a favorite with visitors is the run from Bangkok to Kanchanaburi and Nam Tok. The weekend diesel railcar departs Thonburi station, across the river from Bangkok, at 6:30 AM and returns at 7:30 PM. The train stops at Nakhon Pathom for a short sight-seeing tour and then continues to Kanchanaburi, where it crosses the River Kwai and carries on to Nam Tok, from where a minibus goes to the famous Khao Pang Waterfalls.

It was here, at Kanchanaburi, 80 miles west of Bangkok, where during World War II the infamous "Bridge over the River Kwai" was built as part of the Japanese Death Railway.

The bridge that stands there today is not the same one constructed during the war, which was destroyed by Allied air raids. Nevertheless, tourists still like to walk across it. The graves of thousands of Allied soldiers can also be seen at the cemetery in Kanchanaburi, along with a museum run by

One of the fine old wood-burning train engines is seen here on the track at the site of the infamous Death Railway in Kanchanaburi.

run by Buddhist monks. The museum is no more than a bamboo shed with a thatch roof, an exact replica of the POW camp that had been located on the same spot.

There's one other train journey in Thailand that few people know. It's the train to Mahachai. It departs from Thonburi, the suburb across the river from Bangkok, and takes one hour and fifteen minutes to reach Mahachai, a small town south of Bangkok on the Gulf of Siam. For those who want to see Thailand in a capsule, this is the train to take. It has everything in a nutshell that a long, two-day train journey can offer.

Locating the station in Thonburi is a feat in itself. First you must find the statue of King Taksin, the Siamese general who managed to expel the Burmese and establish a new capital at Thonburi. From the statue you begin walking south, looking down the alleyways until you see in the distance a railway track. Turn down this alley but watch your head. The lane is crammed with shops and food stalls, all under awnings that drown out the sunlight. At the end of the lane you come to the station. Fall in line and buy your ticket, only a few baht for the round trip. The train leaves every hour on the hour.

Your fellow passengers are school children in uniform, monks in saffron robes, vendors with their wares, housewives doing their shopping, everyone you can imagine from old to young, but no tourists.

The train arrives on the narrow track, sounding its whistle for those in the way to clear the line. It comes to a slow stop and in less than five minutes the passengers squeeze out on to the platform, while those waiting shove aboard. Instantly the train is off again, with a noisy clippedy-clap that makes you wonder if this is not the Disneyland Special. It could well be.

From the slum area of Thonburi the train passes through a wall of clapboard shacks, so close that you can reach out and touch them. The shacks are on stilts above a blackened klong that serves as a waterway for those living there.

The train then enters the open rice fields of the south, green and lush, with the train stopping at villages no larger than a city block. As you pass through a village, you can look into the houses, into the very bedrooms. You are looking at rural Thailand close up.

If you return by the next train from Mahachai, you are back to where you began in two and a half hours, much richer and wiser to Thai country life.

If you like taking train journeys to nowhere, then you might consider the Borneo express train to Tenom. It's not an express, and certainly not luxury, but it is different. The trip takes four hours to cover a 100 miles. It's located in Sabah in East Malaysia on the island Borneo. It runs from Kota Kinabalu, the capital, to the small mining town of Tenom buried deep in the jungle. Fellow passengers are likely to be tattooed Muruts with wicker baskets of smelly durians and live chickens tethered to bamboo poles.

The Tenom train has been chugging along ever since it was put into service in the mid 1880s, and it's the only train you can find in Borneo.

There are two types of passenger trains available on the line. The railcars which most tourists take are the best for comfort, speed and views, while the ordinary diesel trains are

The train to Tenom on the island of Borneo cuts a swath through dense jungle. The jounrey takes a jolting four hours to cover an interesting 100 miles.

the ones to take if you want a slower, more colorful journey packed in with the local people and their products. Make your choice before you purchase your ticket.

The railcar is basically an overgrown minibus with just 13 seats. Sit in front on the right side going out from Kota Kinabalu, and on the left coming back from Tenom, as you get the best views of the river and there's a clear view of the narrow track unwinding in front of you.

The train follows the Padas River through steamy jungle. At times the foliage is so dense it forms a tunnel over the narrow track. Monkeys swing through the trees and you almost expect an elephant to block the way. It has happened. Although elephants are not indigenous to Borneo, they were imported by the Sultan of Sulu in the last century and have gone wild.

The railcar turns sharp corners and zips into the rugged hills of the Crocker Range. Passengers put great trust in the little railcar, as it cuts through dark stone tunnels and skirts the awesomely uninviting rapids of the Padas River. At one section I could see white-water rafters in their frail yellow craft swishing down the river. The sport of river rafting has

Passengers aboard the Reunification Express in Vietnam smile for the camera. The train runs between Ho Chi Minh City and Hanoi. Photo Mick Elmore.

even invaded Borneo. We can be thankful it's only rafting. A generation ago it might have been white hunters after elephant or tapir.

The area the Tenom train traverses is what the world's armchair travellers call 'The Interior,' the dark side of Borneo. Until a hundred years ago, when the track was first laid, it was just that—the dark interior. Travelers then had to either hack their way through jungle or negotiate the tumultuous rapids to get where they wanted to go.

Tenom is a hilly inland town where the railway stops and not much happens, unless it's Sunday and the market is open. Even then, unless you are after food for the table there's not much to buy. The people, however, are what make the market places interesting. Nearly everyone poses for photographs.

For your return trip you can go back by rail or else travel by Landrover through Keningau and Tambunan completing a round trip. The Government Rest House at Keningau is a popular stopover for excursions to Murut country.

If you want a touch of Chinese trains, you don't have to go all they way to China. Hong Kong will do. You can take the short two-hour journey from Kowloon to the New Territories, and if you have the pass and proper visas, you can remain aboard the train for its journey into Canton.

The Philippines were once known for excellent train travel, but those days are past. There's only one line left, from Manila to Legaspi, and that may soon close.

While the Philippine railways are passing into oblivion, the railways in Vientiane are sparking into new life. The most popular route here is the Reunification Express between Ho Chi Minh City and Hanoi.

Bangladesh and Burma have interesting railways, but the one that tops all others in Asia is the Toy Train to Darjeeling. The train beings in the town of Siliguri at the foothills of the Himalayas and winds and twists up rugged mountain passes to the hill station at Darjeeling. It's so slow at times you can get out and walk. But speed is not our quest here.

The miniature, coal-burning engine pulls four small passenger-cars over a track of very narrow gauge. When I first saw the train at the station in Siliguri I thought it was a joke, or a transplant from Disneyland. But sure enough, it was real, with real steam and real passengers squeezing into undersized compartments.

Construction on the rail line began in 1879 but not until 1915 did it reach all the way to Siliguri. Before then, all supplies for Darjeeling and all exports from the town had to be transported by bullock cart along the Siliguri road. This road, still known as the Hill Cart Road, was so called because its gradient is such that even bullock carts could climb it.

The whole line is an ingenious feat of engineering and includes four complete loops and five switchbacks, some of which were added after the initial construction had been completed to ease the line's gradient at certain points. One of the most important additions was the Batasia loop on the final descent into Darjeeling. Altogether, there are 132 unsupervised level crossings.

A stern lady conductor, left, checks passengers boarding the Reunionification Express in Vietnam. A reminder of the war in Vietnam, a pillbox stand guard over the railline into Danang. Photos by Mick Elmore.

No Disneyland or Universal City train ride could be more dramatic. The ancient little train engine chugs and groans and spits out steam as if it is about to explode. For 50 miles it continues upwards, not even stopping in many small villages where passengers have to hop off or on to the moving train. The steeper the climb the more ear-shattering becomes the noise as steel grinds against steel, slipping and sliding but never giving in.

After seven hours you round a bend and suddenly Darjeeling is there, built on a hill, with houses and buildings standing on the crests of steep ridges, and in the background looms the snow caps of the rugged Kanchenjunga Range.

Taking the Toy Train to Darjeeling is one thing; taking it back is something else. It's a journey that would make a roller-coaster-ride in an amusement seem mild. When I first boarded the train, I wondered why there were hugh buffers at the end of the line. When I returned I discovered the reason. It's all the brakeman can do to bring the train to a screeching halt at the terminal, and the brakes may not always work.

On the E&O Orient Express you don't have to worry about things like failing breaks and monkeys climbing through windows. It's more of the question like, Should I have another champagne or not?

Chapter 12

THE MOOD OF SOUTHEAST ASIA
Living with Volcanoes and Monsoons

Southeast Asia is a mood as well as a place. It can be bewitching, almost magical. There's something hypnotic about the sound of tiny temple bells tinkling in a breeze, or the chants of Buddhist monks in the still light of dawn. Or the sweet, mist-laden scent of the northern hills of Thailand where the Shan and Karen, and other hilltribes, live. Or the power of the Irrawaddy, or the untameness of the Sunderbans. There's stark naked beauty of the Sulu Islands and the sea gypsies who live there. If you want to feel at peace with the world, climb to the top of a hill station, like Darjeeling, Cameron, Frazier Hill, even Penang Hill—and look out over the landscape at dawn, and stand there when the sun comes up.

There are images so powerful you cannot forget them, ever. I remember a scene on Bali that will always be with me. I was visiting Ubud, the village where artists live, and decided to take a walk into the hills above. I followed a path that lead up a steep climb into the hills. Somewhere far above, I had heard, was a temple. "You must see it," the Balinese told me.

The path led through a thickly wooded area where a forest of banyan trees grew. How magnificent was this forest, perhaps even godly. Banyan trees are beautiful, and they grow with such grandeur. When one sees them for the first time there is little wonder that the Balinese believe that the forests where they grow are sacred. Here in the dark expanse of shade, the legend goes, their gods triumph. The forest, green and damp and heavy with the scent of decay, is especially welcoming in late afternoons, when the tropical sun is most fierce, and here in the cool shade, the world seems to be still. I found a place to sit and rest at the roots of a spreading banyan tree. Pencil-thin shafts of sun light filtered down through the foliage and flecked the forest floor in delicate patches of gold.

The sounds that came to me, at first, were inconsequential,

until I minded them. Birds unseen in the deep foliage above sang cryptically to one another. There were sounds of insects, unfamiliar, suddenly breaking the stillness, loud and shrill at first, and then stopping, abruptly as they began. A dog yapping, barely audible, was heard in a distant village. An occasional leaf fluttered earthward, catching a ray of slanted light, disappeared and reappeared until it became lost among purple shadows beyond.

When you sit there long enough, you wonder if your senses are deceiving you, as I wondered when I heard, very faintly, the echo of a gong somewhere far off. A gong in the forest! In an instant more, it was clearer, and louder, and mingled now with faraway voices. Then came the sound of a flute, and another, and more gongs. The yapping of the dog that seemed so distant was now closer, and grew louder. My peace and joy of the forest were being disturbed by something strange and bewildering, something mysterious and unfathomable, as Bali itself is, especially for one like me who was a stranger to the island.

And as I sat there, my back pressed against the knurled roots of the banyan tree, perplexed and uncertain, and the sounds grew more distinct, there came into view far down the sun-flecked path, a column of marchers, led by men and boys. I watched them grow from fuzzy silhouettes into focus, like a camera zooming in on its subject. I could see them clearly now, all wearing sarongs, white sarongs, and around their waists were scarlet cummerbunds fastened with rich buckles carved in gold. They wore headbands, these too all white, and pointed at the crown. Those in the lead carried towering bamboo poles, bent over in sweeping arches by the weight of flowing pennants attached to their ends. More marchers followed, boys carrying gaily colored umbrellas suspended high above their heads on long slender poles. The music, gongs and flutes, accompanied by a chorus of singing, grew louder and louder in intensity until it became almost deafening.

Young children ran with the dogs along side the procession, laughing and shouting and calling out to one another, adding to the noise and cacophony of sound. The procession passed, the music and singing dinned, gradually, and presently a line of women in single file came up behind the marchers. Unlike the men who wore white, they were dressed in brightly colored batik sarongs, and in place of head bands like the men wore, they carried upon their heads towering pillars of food, some with tiny plated baskets, heaped with cakes and sweets, and others with tropical fruit. These I learned later were offerings to the gods, and what I was witnessing was a religious procession heading to one of their temples further up the mountain side. It was like a stage, a play that had been conducted for me, and for me alone. No one even noticed me.

Was this truly man being in tune with nature?

That same evening I was invited to dine in Ubud at the home of my friend, Dutch painter Han Snel. It was evening when I arrived. It's a magnificent house, where Han lives with his Balinese wife. He had it constructed from red brick and gray volcanic stone, patterned after the feudal palace of Prince Tjokorde Agung.

We sat and had a drink on an open pavilion, where long shadows from torches crept out over the carved stone walls. We talked about Balinese life, small talk, about the procession I saw that day, until dinner was announced. A servant led us to another pavilion at a lower level, also lighted by torch. Somewhere in the deep darkness a *gamelan* orchestra played. So softly and finely did they perform that I could not help wondering if they were not part of the night. The meal was excellent, native dishes, a rare delight, and occasionally I had to glance about to remind myself that my host was not a myth, that this was all real. The meal lasted until the late hours. The music continued; the wine flowed; the mood was like I had never known before. It was real, and this *is* Southeast Asia.

The very first travelers to Southeast Asia were spellbound

by it's strange mood. Seamen who visited the area called it "the land below the winds." Technically speaking, with the exception of the Philippines, it is free of typhoons and other such violent tropical storms. This doesn't mean, however, that tropical Southeast Asia is without natural calamities. It is a land of monsoons and dramatic volcanoes, both of which can be devastating at times. And both which create a mood. What power a volcano has, especially one that sends up clouds of ash 10,000 feet into the sky and looks like its about to explode.

Perhaps nature's most spectacular, and awesome, sight is that of an exploding volcano. I witnessed one such volcanic eruption from the deck of my schooner *Third Sea* in the Santa Cruz Islands. It was a terrifying experience to watch it the way we did.

It happened at night, on one of those black, evil nights when there is no moon. It was impossible to tell where the sky and sea met. For all practical purposes, we were traveling through a black, velvet void. The only light was the dim, red glow of the binnacle reflected on the face of the helmsman. It's eerie sailing on nights like this, when the sails are set and the schooner heels into unseen seas. The only sane thing, it seems, is the compass, which points out the course.

We knew we were nearing the Santa Cruz Islands in the Western Pacific, and that out there coming up on our starboard was a small dot which on the chart read Tinakulu Volcano. We gave it a wide berth by several miles.

Suddenly in the blackness of night there was an explosion, and shortly afterwards the sky turned crimson and then a fiery red. Belching clouds of smoke bolted skyward, followed by a rumble that seemed to come from the core of the earth. Those of the crew who were below deck scrambled topside, and we all stood dumbfounded, uncertain. Was the earth disintegrating before our eyes? Twisting balls of fire hurled upwards like rockets out of control, and sparks and flames spewed umbrella-like into the surrounding sea.

Only when we saw the white-hot lava flowing down the

cone-shaped slopes did we realize we were witnessing a volcano erupting. In those few brief moments we felt the god-awful fury that would certainly prevail if the earth did explode. It wasn't a satisfying feeling.

For the next twenty minutes we lined the deck, not knowing if it was the beauty of the spectacle or the fear of it that kept us spellbound at the rail. Then, as suddenly as it had begun, it ended.

When dawn came and we looked astern at the still silhouette of Tinakulu, it all seemed strangely unreal. Had the volcano really erupted? There were no other islands about, no other ships. We were the only witnesses. Then, as we sailed ever so slowly away, and Tinakulu vanished into the blue of the sea and sky, we wondered if even the very mountain existed at all.

The incident deeply impressed me and it made me realize how we who live in Southeast Asia also live in the shadow of volcanoes, and more often than not we are only dimly aware of them.

Most of my life I have been chasing these wonders of nature. I fell in love with the first one I ever saw, climbed it,

Volcanoes have a magic all their own, and give Southeast Asia its mood. The area has 850 volcanoes of which Indonesia has 167. Many are still active.

and thereafter had to climb those that crossed my path. There is something challenging about volcanoes, which makes one want to climb them. They have a magnetic force, a force that draws you towards them, that makes you want to stand on their summits and perhaps become akin with nature. Maybe they satisfy our need to conquer, not nature, but fear. Volcanoes are often beautiful, but they are always awesome — simply by virtue of their existence.

I was in my teens when I first saw Mount Vesuvius in southern Italy. I went to see the ruins at Pompeii and, when I saw the volcano majestically rising in the background, I had to climb the mountain. I was enthralled all the way to the summit, and I believed Vesuvius to be the most beautiful mountain in the world.

I was also to learn that volcanoes bring destruction. Pompeii was a flourishing city under the Roman Empire until early one morning in 79 AD Mount Vesuvius became angry and blew her top. While the people slept, she dropped thousands of tones of ash and cinders which completely covered Pompeii. The inhabitants died where they slept, and so complete was the destruction that nearly 2000 years were to pass before the ruins were uncovered.

My next real adventure with a volcano was Mount Popocatepetl in Mexico.

I went to Mexico City one summer to do graduate work at the university, and being a student with little funds, and a wife and two small children, I had to rent a flat on the eighth floor of an apartment building. The building had no lift and, with Mexico City at 8,500 feet above sea level, it was exhausting work climbing the stairs, especially with baby carriages and groceries. At every level we would rest.

There were windows at all the levels, but in the summer Mexico City is clouded and smog-filled and there is not much to see. One afternoon, however, the air was clear. I stopped at the eighth floor, looked out and couldn't quite believe my eyes. There before me was the most splendid sight imaginable.

Far in the distance, rising above other mountains in the range, were two snow-capped peaks that I immediately recognized from photographs—Mount Popocatepetl and Mount Ixtaccihuatl, both around 18,000 feet high. In Central and Latin America, only the extinct volcano Cerro Aconcagua in Chile is higher.

The view of these two mountains was hypnotic. I couldn't take my eyes away from them, especially Mount Popocatepetl, a perfect cone, and perhaps even more beautiful than Vesuvius. Then and there I made up my mind to climb the mountain. I began training.

The climb up Mount Popo, as it is called by those who know it, is more than a Sunday hike. It takes careful planning, with full mountain-climbing gear—ice axes, crampons, ropes, cold weather clothing. Nevertheless, I made the arrangements and two months later made my first attempt with two other students from the university. We were unsuccessful. We were less than 1,200 feet from the crater when a fierce lightning storm forced us to abandon the mountain. A month later a second attempt put us at the lower rim of the crater, but so dense was the cloud bank, and so thick the sulfur fumes, that we could not make the final distance to the top of the rim.

Four years passed before I returned to make a third attempt. We started the climb at 3 AM at 12,000 feet (3,692 meters.) Every step was a struggle, every breath an effort. Dawn came at 16,000 feet (4,900 meter).

We reached the snow line and put our crampons on. The sun came up and the glare on frozen snow became blinding. Boots feel like lead weights. Each step was a victory in itself. Step, step, one more step. Suddenly there were no more steps. The summit! We had reached the summit.

The sight is frightening. It's all hell and ugly. There's little beauty looking down into the evil depths of a boiling crater. The walls are sheer. Fifteen hundred feet to the bottom. Foul! Gaseous yellow smoke rises from every crevasse and every crack. But still, we reached the summit. It was noon.

The very top of the mountain was all rock and windswept, with a metal cross, and far below us lay the great Valley of Mexico. We made it!

Mount Popocatepetl is the highest volcano I have scaled, but it wasn't the most dramatic climb. I reserve that distinction for Mount Agung on Bali. Here truly is a mountain with mood.

Until 1963, the Balinese believed that Mount Agung was extinct. It was the same year that Eka Dasa Ruda, the greatest of all Bali-Hindu sacrifices, was to take place. The sacrifice had not been held for two centuries and was scheduled for March 8th. On the morning of the celebrations people who were working on the preparations saw a yellow glare rising from the mountain, but no one was unduly alarmed. Devotees continued to gather around Besakih Temple at the foot of the mountain, and while the high priests began the animal sacrifices the mountain rumbled and thick columns of smoke rose from the crater. Old people shook their heads: their mountain had been dormant since 1350.

A few minutes before noon there was an explosion and soon lava began to flow down the slopes of Mount Agung.

A statue in stone appears on a lonely hillside on the island of Bali while Mount Agung looms up high in the backround. The volcano last erupted in 1963.

There were more explosions and the lava flow turned into rivers of molten rock. The Balinese who were watching in awe now had to drop everything and flee for their lives. By afternoon entire villages were under the flow and bridges had been swept away. The rumbling and the lava flow continued for several days. Today only the uppermost parts of Besakih Temple protrude above the hardened lava.

The climb to the summit of Mount Agung is a soul-searching experience. The mountain is still hot and smoke rises from crevasses, and occasionally muffled rumbles echo from somewhere deep within. You feel that you are treading on sacred ground, and you dare not move a stone or rock for fear it may anger the gods. Mount Agung does strange things to you.

Indonesia has the greatest concentration of active volcanoes in the world. Worldwide, including submarine volcanoes, there is a total of 850, 167 of which are in Indonesia. Seventy-seven of these have erupted in modern times. But it isn't only Indonesia that has active volcanoes; most of the Malay archipelago, which includes the Philippines,

Volcanos create a mood, and no island in the world has more mood than Bali. Balinese believe their gods and goddess reside in the mountains.

is still an active region in which islands formed by volcanic activity constantly appear and disappear. Sailing through these waters is a navigational hazard. I've spotted islands that don't appear on the charts, and when I asked natives about them, they explained: "They came up out of the sea one night!"

Hardly a week goes by when you don't read about a volcano erupting in the Philippines. Mount Mayon, southeast of Manila, has erupted 44 times in the last four centuries. In September 1984, 28,000 people in the town of Santo Domingo, six miles from Mount Mayon, had to flee from their homes as flaming lava headed towards their town in the latest eruption.

New Britain Island, north of New Guinea, is another active region. I sailed *Third Sea* into Rabaul, the capital, to find myself surround by smoking volcanoes. And when I climbed one and looked down at the bay, I could see the bay itself was the crater of a large volcano that exploded eons ago and that the smaller volcanoes were but minor recent eruptions.

Volcanologists, who keep a close study of the region, fear that any one of the volcanoes can go any time. In the short

One of the most active volcano regions in the world is on the chain of islands that make up New Guinea and Indonesia. Above, a menacing volcano looms up in the background on New Britain Island.

time I spent anchored in Rabaul, I felt a number of violent shocks, some of which rattled the dishes on the table at a home in which I was dining.

In 1937, two volcanoes in the harbor, Mautupi and Vulcan, did erupt. The eruptions caused darkness for several days and showered the waters for kilometers around with ash and pumice stones. A 5000-ton freighter was sucked into one of the erupting cones and disappeared with the loss of all crew. Days after the eruption, a returning ship plowed through pumice up to ten feet deep. The hull was polished down to bare metal by the floating sea of stones.

In modern times, the greatest explosion from a volcanic eruption occurred at Krakatoa, an island in the Sunda Strait between Java and Sumatra. I intended to visit the island aboard my schooner but couldn't arrange a sailing permit with the Indonesian government.

When Krakatoa erupted in 1863, it literally shook the world. In the space of less than 48 hours, the island blew up in a series of explosions that were felt around the world and could be heard 'like the roar of heavy guns' on the island of

Rabaul on New Britain was built on the rim of a geat volcano that erupted 60 million years ago. The Japanese held Rabual throughout World War II. A Japanese Zero on a hill overlooking the harbor is a reminder of the war.

167

Rodrigues, 3,150 miles (5,040 kilometers) away. Rocks were thrown 30 miles (46 kilometers) high. A total of 163 villages were wiped out and 36,380 were killed as a direct result of the eruption. For many days afterwards, much of Java was in total darkness and the sea for hundreds of miles was paved with pumice stone.

For several years afterwards, the entire earth's weather patterns were altered. Millions of tons of dust floated in the skies and fallout was felt in London for two years. When the eruptions subsided, half the island had disappeared, the peak was split in two, and cinders and ash were 150 feet (46 meters) deep. Not one seed or spore of life of any kind survived.

A year later, a visitor to Krakatoa made an extended search for plant or animal life. He found a spider but nothing else on the still-hot lava beds. Three years later it was reported that grass was growing on the lowlands and flowering plants and ferns appeared inland.

Krakatoa became a botanist's Mecca. Here scientists could study the birth of an island and jungle life. Only fifty years after Krakatoa had been destroyed, trees were 150 feet tall and had spread two-thirds of the way up the mountain slope. Today, the island is covered with primary jungle.

Krakatoa may have had the greatest explosion in modern times, but the greatest eruption was that of Tambora, a volcano on the island of Sumbawa, also in Indonesia. The volcano erupted in 1815, blew open a crater seven miles wide and lowered the height of the island by 1000 yards. It was about four times greater than the Krakatoa eruption.

Volcanic eruptions on Java are commonplace today. There are long periods when the Singapore skyline is clouded over from volcanic dust carried north by the prevailing winds. A commercial airliner lost power in all four jet engines when the plane ran into a thick cloud of volcanic dust. Fortunately the pilot was able to restart the engines before the plane plummeted to earth.

A volcanic island that will forever excite me is New

Zealand's North Island. To arrive in Auckland by air is a most enthralling experience. When I close my eyes, the vision becomes complete. The plane approaches at dawn's first light, mountain ranges capped in clouds, with volcanoes shaped like inverted cones, appear, and the island, deep in long shadows, hazy and irregular, seems to be floating upon an ebony sea. New Zealand, in the half light, seems almost prehistoric.

In Auckland's suburban area alone there are 38 volcanoes. Geologists date the oldest to be approximately 36,000 years old. The last one to explode was Rangitoto in 1150. The most powerful volcano to blow her top was Taupo in 130 AD. In one mighty explosion more than 30,000 million tons of pumice, moving at 400 miles an hour (640 kilometers), entered the atmosphere. It flattened an area of 8,000 square miles. According to the experts, Auckland is ready for another eruption within the next thirty years.

Necessity makes South Sea islanders live on volcanic islands where, unlike coral atolls, the soil is fertile. But for the New Zealander to build his house on top of a volcano is nothing short of madness. I was invited to one such home, owned by an eccentric movie producer. The house was actually constructed above a volcano, which the owner said was dormant, even though it continued to smoke. The producer used the crater to full advantage. Chambers deep below served as storage and recreation rooms. It was all very eerie and made for good parties late at night. The house helped his image.

I visited another house that truly captured the thrill of living on a volcano. The mountain was a thirty-two mile (51 kilometer) drive from Auckland, and the last two miles we had to walk. The path led through a thickly wooded forest, with steps carved into black volcanic rock the final hundred yards.

At the top of the stairs, we arrived at the house which stood at the edge of the crater. It was constructed solidly out of stone and wood, with wings and a glassed-in verandah facing the valley from which we climbed. The slopes dropped steep on all sides and were green and wooded. Mist and fog rose from below and seeped up through the trees. White birds fluttered through distant foliage.

The interior of the house had a living room with the largest fireplace I had ever seen. It was the crater itself. To light a fire all one had to do was slide logs to the edge of the opening and they would ignite. The owner of this fabulous place was a noted potter, Jeff Scholes. His studio faced the valley where the view is always inspiring, and his kiln was the crater. The place, to say the least, was exciting. Any minute you might expect the volcano to erupt.

People who live in the shadow of volcanoes, and the many New Zealanders who live on volcanoes, experience a kind of Russian-roulette existence. They defend their position and tell you that the risk is minor. An old-timer in Rabaul laughed when I asked him if he minded living beneath the rim of smoking volcanoes. "Not at all," he insisted. "Volcanoes erupt on average every fifty years around Rabaul, and that's a long time in between."

"When was the last one?" I asked.

"In 1937, around fifty years ago," he answered and smiled.

And that leaves us with monsoons. What is a monsoon, anyway? Most people believe it's a rain, but that's not correct. I remember a course of study at the School of Foreign Service at Georgetown University. It wasn't an easy course. Professor James Hunter gave an hour's discussion on what the students could expect for the coming semester. He concluded by saying, "One sure way to fail this course is to call a monsoon a rain. It isn't a rain; it's a wind. Don't forget it." I never forgot it. A monsoon is not a rain, but a wind.

A monsoon is more than a wind, however. For anyone who hasn't lived in a monsoon belt, the very name 'monsoon' has a way of spelling romance. It has appeared in the title of books, plays and songs. *The Rains Came* was a movie box office hit in the 1930s. The author who was clever enough not to misuse the term monsoon was Louis Bromfield. He never mentioned monsoons but he managed to leave readers with the feeling that when the winds blew someone was going to get wet.

My own experience with monsoon winds came long before I studied under Professor Hunter at Georgetown, when I was in school in Peking, or Beijing as it is called today. In Peking every winter the winds come down from the wastes of Mongolia and play havoc on the city. The monsoon wind there is well known, not only for its power, which the peasants used to their advantage by attaching sails to their wheel barrows, but also for the dust it brings with it from the great Gobi Desert.

It was a harsh, penetrating dust that came upon the helpless city like a plague. Sometimes for days the swirling dark mass would block out the sun. It was impossible to walk through the streets of Peking without ending up with bloodshot eyes and a need for a bath. Even padded doors and double window sashes were powerless to withstand the scourge. In my room I would shake the dust from my blankets after I dressed for school each morning.

Monsoons begin with a distant cloud on the horizon, and unlike popular belief, you can't set your watch by a coming monsoon. They stirke suddenly, without warning. Right, the best assurance in Southeast Asia is to carry an umbrella.

But it never brought rain.

Outside of Asia, there are many such types of monsoon winds around the world, winds that have nothing to do with rain. When the infamous foehn blows in the Alps in Switzerland, it is said to cast a spell on the people in certain villages. When a crime is committed during the presence of a foehn, a judge will often be considerate, and in many cases he may even dismiss the charges against the accused.

Then there is a sirocco of the Sahara and the Ghibli of the Libyan Desert, where the wind has the force of a blast furnace and super heats the ground temperature to 130 degrees and over. During a Ghibli nothing moves, but there is no rain, only sand and heat.

Monsoons may exist in places all over the world but Asia is traditionally known as the land of the monsoons. When the monsoon winds blow here, you can be certain rain will come.

The name monsoon was given by the Arabs, and it means nothing more than a seasonal wind. In other words, any wind that seasonally reverses its direction can be termed a monsoon. The cause of the change is due to the difference of annual temperature traits over land and sea. The monsoon blows from cold to warm regions; from sea toward land in summer; from land toward sea in the winter. It's the sudden change in temperature that causes rain to fall.

Somewhere long ago, I read it was possible to set one's watch by the coming of the monsoon. When I came to Southeast Asia I learned nothing can be further from the truth. The most unpredictable wind is the monsoon. Unfortunately, the welfare of Asian countries depends upon this uncertain economic factor—the monsoons which bring rain for their crops. Bihar State in India, for example, had insufficient rainfall for three years straight, and nearly three million people faced death. Wheat shipments from the West saved many lives. The following year, the monsoon came early, and with such fury and violence, the rain flooded the land. The whole state was declared a disaster. Dr. Vijayenra Rad, former director of the Indian Institute of Economics, summed it up best. He said, "The Indian economy is a gamble in rainfall."

In Southeast Asia the monsoon has become synonymous with rainfall. The seasonal winds here almost always bring rain, and the region has become known as a "monsoon belt," with an annual rainfall of at least 100 inches per year. The question that comes to mind is how much is a 100 inches of rainfall? Weather men conclude that any region with a rainfall of less ten inches or more than 60 inches is said to be an extreme. Both London and Paris have an average rainfall of 25 inches per year. New York City and Sydney are wetter, with averages of 45 inches.

One of the wettest spots on earth caused by monsoon rains is Cherrapunji in Assam. Overlooking the valley of Surma in Bangladesh, the average annual rainfall here is 425 inches. It has been known to rain 20 inches in a single day, with 529 inches holding the record for any one given year. In France it would take 25 years for the same amount of rain to fall. Only one other place on earth has a greater rainfall than Cherrapunji, and that is Mt. Waialali on the island of Hawaii. The average yearly rainfall on this dormant volcano is 460 inches, although the rains are not brought on by a monsoon.

Scientists have come up with a new theory on the origin of monsoons. They claim that monsoons originate over land, as far away as Saudi Arabia in the Middle East, and not over the Indian Ocean as commonly believed. The evidence for the theory came from data they generated while making geographical surveys of the Arabian Sea aboard the American research vessel *Oceanographer*. Scientists took atmospheric measurements of radon, a radioactive gas resulting from the disintegration of radium. Radon is released only by soil, not by water.

While scientists may probe the atmosphere looking for the origins of monsoons, we are fortunate to have poets, writers and travelers in Asia who look upon monsoons with romance, and yet, regardless of how much has been written, said or quoted about monsoons, one thing we can be certain–no one has ever seen a monsoon. What they see is the rain. English poet Percy Shelley reminds us that.

Who can see the wind?
Neither you nor I
But when the trees
Bow down their heads,
The wind is passing by.
And I won't ever forget; a monsoon is not a rain.

Chapter 13

THE MYSTERIOUS ORIENT
Lost Tribes and Jungle Giants

The mysterious Orient! Black Magic! Spells! Witch doctors? Elusive natives of the rain forest! Jungle giants? Lost Cities! The mysteries of the Far East!

What are these phenomen everyone associates with the East? Do we accept the premise that such mysteries exist, and if we do, are they real, or imagined? Is not Southeast Asia, really, a mood, a mood that's to be felt and not necessarily understood?

No adventure in the Southeast Asia would be complete without some involvement with the so-called 'mysteries of the Orient'. I remember when I was quite young I read a short story by Somerset Maugham, about an Englishman who had spent a lifetime running a rubber estate in Malaya. When the time came for him to retire, he packed his bags, boarded a steamer and set sail for England. Behind he left not only a way of life but also a Malay woman with whom he had spent most of his years in the East. The woman was not too pleased with his departure, so she had a *bomoh,* a Malay witch doctor, put a curse on him. The unfortunate Englishman, the story goes, died from hiccups before he reached England. It was a fascinating story, but, I thought then, a bit ridiculous. How could someone put a curse upon someone else, and have him die of hiccups? Ridiculous. It was all part of Maugham's imagination. But when I came to Asia, I learned that the noted English writer had traveled widely throughout the Malay States and from his everyday experiences he drew the plots for his stories. The stories were more real than imagined. I also discovered that some very strange things do go on in Asia, and I learned that if you want to survive in this part of the world, you cannot let yourself become a diehard skeptic, or even a doubter. You soon learn to accept those mysteries that once may have baffled you. You may not totally believe them, but you accept them.

The learning process is slow. It doesn't happen in a week or a month, or even in a year. But it does happen, eventually, if you remain in Asia long. It begins when you go to a Thaipusam celebration at the Batu Caves in Malaysia, and see things performed by Hindu devotees which even in your wildest imagination you never thought humanly possible. Or when you travel to the Philippines during the Easter holidays, and on Friday morning visit Batangas outside Manila and watch believers being nailed to a cross, and later see them kneeling in church praying. And when you hear and perhaps visit with a *bomoh,* or a soothsayer or rain-stopper, or a medium or faith-healer, you know it's all an inherent part of the mysterious Orient.

Andy Larson, a friend who used to live in Kuala Lumpur and was married to a lovely Chinese woman from Hong Kong, came to Asia with some fixed ideas. He wasn't the type to be worried by the number thirteen; he wouldn't hesitate to walk under a ladder; he wasn't alarmed if a black cat crossed his path. Nothing fazed him. Being a determined backwoods Canadian, his philosophy was "show me."

At the time of the incident I am about to relate, Andy was head of a large advertising firm in Kuala Lumpur, one of the biggest in Asia. He had a responsible position, and he wasn't apt to be led astray by buffoonery. He wouldn't have been where he was if he had been.

I was sitting in Andy's office one afternoon, having a coffee, when our conversation lead to a story that had appeared in the *Straits Times* the same morning. It mentioned something about a law that was about to be passed requiring *bomohs* to register their services. It seems there were too many quacks in the witch doctor business. Andy casually leaned back in his chair, and said, "Let me tell you about a *bomoh I* met when I first came to Malaysia." Before beginning his story, he explained how the incident changed his thinking.

Andy had a Malaysian Chinese secretary, an attractive,

intelligent woman, who had been distraught about something. "For the past few months she was not the happy, carefree girl she once had been," he said.

Then one day Andy noticed a change in her. She came into the office for dictation, all smiles. "What's the occasion?" he asked her.

"I have a second meeting with the *bomoh* this evening," she said jovially.

"You have what?"

She repeated she was going to see her *bomoh*.

Andy then explained to me a few things about *bomohs,* that they can be Malay, Indian or Chinese, male or female. The *bomoh* the secretary was going to visit was an Indian gentleman.

"But why?" Andy asked.

"To break the spell," she said, and then for the next ten minutes she proceeded to explain to her wide-eyed boss about the spell.

She maintained the spell was put upon her by a young man with whom she had had a love affair a few years previously. When she broke off the relationship, the jilted lover became irate and threatened her. She remained persistent, however, and refused to see or have anything to do with him. The man swore he would get even with her. He then went and hired the services of a *bomoh,* who put a curse upon the girl. The witch doctor maintained that she would never have a successful love affair again.

Andy had to admit, there was some truth to the matter. He was strangely aware that although the his secretary was good-looking, neat and with a pleasant personality, she had no boyfriends. If a boy did take her out, he never asked her for a date the second time. Andy thought something was wrong but could never figure it out.

The pretty secretary learned from her friends that there was in Kuala Lumpur a Hindu sect whose priests could remove spells. She went to one of the meetings and met a head priest.

She explained her predicament, and he agreed to help her. He consulted a thumb-worn book of heavenly bodies, found a time that corresponded with a certain phase of the moon and instructed her to return in eleven days. But first, she must buy a small green lime, put it under her mattress during this period and bring it with her when she returned.

She did exactly as she was told: she bought a small green lime, kept it under her mattress for eleven days and with the moon being exactly right she told Andy that this was the night she was to meet the *bomoh*.

What could Andy say? She was dead serious, and he, her boss, was skeptical. Seeing that Andy had his doubts, she said, if he wished, he could accompany her that night. He accepted the invitation.

Andy met his secretary that evening and they drove to a section of town he had not visited before. They parked and followed a narrow, unlit street to a ramshackle building, lit by oil lamps, with a dozen people crowded inside. Others waited outside on the steps. Discordant Indian music, mostly from drums and clanging cymbals, mingled with the chanting of Hindu worshippers, came from within the building. Andy and his secretary entered. The head priest was already in a trance, as were most of the others there.

It was strange and mystifying, Andy explained. Suddenly someone next to him slipped into a trance and began rolling on the floor, while others, already on the floor, shook violently as though suffering from an epileptic fit. A young Indian girl had to be carried out of the building. Andy's first impulse was to flee, but he felt duty-bound to remain.

After the ceremony had been going on for half an hour, several assistants took hold of the priest, pulled out his tongue and shoved several long spikes through it. The wounds bled only a moment. They took the blood and dotted his bare chest and forehead, which was then smeared with red ochre and ashes.

Supposedly, the high priest was taken over by a Hindu

god. He was led to an altar, whereupon devotees lined up in front of him and revealed their problems.

Andy's secretary was among them. She gave him the lime, which he cut in half, and then pulled from it a tiny piece of dirty rag. He explained to the bewildered girl that this was once a piece of her clothing that the jilted boyfriend had used in the ritual to put the spell upon her. Thus he had removed the spell.

"Then what happened?" I asked Andy.

"You wouldn't believe it," he began, "but her life changed drastically. In fact, so much so that I lost her." He explained that only a few short weeks after the meeting with the *bomoh,* she became engaged to a young Chinese man who was departing for Australia. They married and she and her husband settled in Sydney. Andy still gets greeting cards from her from time to time.

Anyone who spends time in Malaysia is certain to hear village tales about *bomohs,* but it isn't always restricted to villages. *Bomohs* travel in royal and government circles and they play an integral role in Malay society.

The main task of a *bomoh* is healing. By autosuggestion he falls into a trance and spirits speak through his words. The results achieved by these *bomohs* have baffled doctors and scientists the world over.

Perhaps the most famous, or at least the most publicized, *bomohs* in Malaysia are the rain-stoppers. Many countries profess to have rain-makers, but few have rain-stoppers. The event can be a very serious affair.

A famous woman *bomoh* was engaged to keep rain away during a royal wedding. It seems it had rained continuously for a week before the wedding, and finally the royal family engaged Che Lamah, known for her ability to stop rain. For five days, without bathing, she kept up incantations during the ceremony. For the five days, throughout the wedding, the weather was fine.

One of the best known rain-stoppers is *bomoh* Lebai

Abdullah bin Omar, who baffled thousands of spectators at a cricket match in Kuala Lumpur in 1962. It was the beginning of the rainy season. Selangor and All Malaya were playing the Commonwealth cricket team for three days.

The Malay Cricket Association engaged Lebai from Kuala Lipis. He had the reputation of having kept the rains away for the Merdeka football tournament. For two days he remained in concealment, in constant meditation. On the afternoon of the third day he came out onto the playing field to the thunderous applause of thousands of spectators. For the three days no rain had fallen on the field, although there was rain in the surrounding areas.

He then untied a knot in a handkerchief he pulled from his pocket. Rain clouds darkened the sky. Members of the team rushed up to him and offered congratulations—before they got wet.

There was a great deal of discussion during some serious floods in Kuala Lumpur a few years back. Residents believed there had been too many cricket matches and official functions for which *bomohs* were called upon to halt the rain. The rains had stored up, and when they fell so came the floods.

Bomohs are also skilled, it's said, in the art of preparing charms to engender love, beauty and courage, to protect against spiritual or material hurt, to prevent girls from marrying rivals, to obtain good business, to shatter a competitor's business, and so forth. Name it and a *bomoh* can probably do it.

But it's not always easy. In preparing certain charms, especially love charms, the potion must be mixed with blood— blood from the corpse of a person who has died violently.

Or suppose you discover your cup of tea is poisoned, and you have already drunk from it. A good *bomoh* will recommend the following: take two dry walnuts, some clean figs, twenty leaves of rue, and 'bruise' and beat together with a dash of salt and seven different kinds of flowers. Take orally immediately.

Another antidote for poison, if the above doesn't work, is burnt tigers' whiskers in coconut oil, which must be licked from a betel leaf. This can also be taken as an internal remedy for chronic rheumatism.

'Bomoh' is a Malay word which means 'medicine man'. In its broader sense it may even be attributed to a medical doctor. As there are different types of doctors, there are different types of *bomohs*.

A Malay *bomoh* may fall into the same classification as a surgeon, physician, gynecologist, dental surgeon or orthopedist. When you desire the services of a *bomoh,* you seek out the one who specializes in your need.

There is, of course, no recognized course of study to guide them. They depend upon the teachings of the elder *bomoh*. Meditation is one of the basic arts practiced by almost every *bomoh*. Each has his own way of chanting incantations, but the substance is basically the same.

Spell-casting is done in the strictest secrecy. It's commonly believed the person wishing the spell cast will ultimately suffer if the charm has been placed for evil or wrong purposes. The *bomoh* is never to blame.

The Hindu festival of Thaipusam involves a form of self-

A Hindi devotee, left, drives spikes through her cheeks in the annual Thaipusam festival in Malaysia. On Good Friday celebration in a small town near Manila the Philippines', a young woman, right. is nailed to the cross.

hypnosis that has to be seen to be believed. I came to know and understand something about it through a Tamil named Mohan who worked for me when I was building my schooner *Third Sea* in Singapore. But first, let me tell you something about this strange Hindu belief.

Thaipusam falls on the day the star Pusam is ascendant in the period of Thai between January and February. It is without doubt the grandest, and most awesome, of Hindu festivals celebrated in Singapore and Malaysia to honor Lord Subramaniam, son of Siva. Hundreds of Hindus who seek penance and absolution for past sins, or who wish to show gratitude to their God for blessings during the year, vow to carry a *kavadi*—a wooden frame decorated with flowers and fruits and supported by long thin spikes pinned or driven into the carrier's body. To do so they go on a strict vegetarian diet for forty days prior to the festival.

Other devotees may have their tongues and cheeks pierced with spikes. Some spikes are more like long rods, ten or twelve feet long and as thick as a man's thumb. These are forced through his cheeks and he walks along holding the rod in his teeth, supported on both sides by his hands. Devotees insist their minds are on their gods and they do not feel pain. Nor do their wounds bleed. And, most unbelievable, there are no scars afterwards.

Singapore celebrates Thaipusam, but the largest gathering is at the Batu Caves north of Kuala Lumpur. Kavadi carriers gather there before dawn, bathe in the river and enter a trance like religious euphoria before mounting the 272 steps to Lord Subramaniam's shrine within the gigantic caves. As many as 100,000 worshipers come to join in the solemn procession.

Inside the cave, where pencil-thin shafts of sunlight shoot down hundreds of meters from cracks in the limestone ceiling, a dozen white-clad priests tend to the thousands of worshipers and bestow upon them blessings and sacred ash.

Spikes from their cheeks are removed, the *kavadis* are lifted, the trance subsides. A coconut is dashed to the ground and camphor is burned. The holy vow made to their God has been fulfilled.

My Tamil worker, Mohan, agreed to carry a *kavadi* at Thaipusam to enable me to complete my schooner on time. It was January, a month before Thaipusam. The schooner was almost complete, and the most important and critical day of construction was nearing. *Third Sea* was built by a special process called ferro-cement construction. Everything hinges on the final day when the entire hull of the vessel must be plastered within the short span of a few hours. Our problem arose when a delay in procuring building material held up the completion date, and put us into the rainy season.

"It will take another two months until the rainy season ends," Mohan said.

"There's not much we can do," I said. We had put up protection around the hull, but unfortunately wet mortar had to be carried through an exposed area. And every day, almost without fail, the rain had been falling. After telling Mohan and the others this, I laughed, and then added: "Maybe we should hire a Malay *bomoh,* a rain-stopper."

Mohan didn't think it was funny and asked if he could take the afternoon off. I agreed and the next day he returned. "We can plaster as scheduled," he said. "It won't rain."

"You have to be kidding!" I said.

"It won't rain," he insisted. "I have asked my gods to help."

I knew not to joke with him now. We plastered the hull as scheduled, and it didn't rain. Mohan had made an agreement with his gods. What I didn't know was that he had agreed that if it didn't rain he would carry a *kavadi* and at the same time let his assistants drive a rod through his cheeks during that coming Thaipusam at the Batu Caves. I and my crew went to the Batu Caves to witness him go through his ordeal.

At four o'clock in the morning we were at the riverbank. We watched Mohan strip and bathe in the river. He was already in a trance and didn't take any notice of us. The air was hypnotic. The beat of the Hindu drums was mesmerizing. I felt myself almost slipping off into a trance and for a moment I was fearful that I might let myself be subjected to spikes entering my body.

I snapped back to reality when I saw Mohan's assistants place the heavy *kavadi* upon his shoulders, supported by skewers that entered his back and chest, followed by the long rod they drove through his cheeks. It was almost too horrifying to watch, but we could hardly turn away. He registered no sign of pain, nor did he wince during the operation. Not a drop of blood came from his wounds.

We stepped aside to let him pass. He was in another world. We followed with the stream of pilgrims who flooded the roadside. The smell of incense filled the air.

Towering above us the massive limestone outcrop turned from an opaque silhouette to a gray specter as the sky paled. Under a gateway hanging with strings of colored bulbs that illuminated the path, the gigantic staircase led to the sacred caves above.

We followed Mohan up the stairs, suffering with him, wondering what it all meant. We lost him in the crowd, and found him again. The steel rod had been removed from his cheeks, and the *kavadi* taken away. There was sacred ash smeared on his cheeks where the rod had pierced his flesh, but there was no wound. He saw us, and a look of surprise came to his face. "You came," he said, pleased, and then added: "It didn't rain."

It didn't rain, and Mohan saw *Third Sea* completed before it sailed on to adventure in Southeast Asia. A simple Hindu devotee, and yet in his mysterious way he helped make it all possible. But then in Asia, we learn, anything is possible.

When I become involved in conversations with Asian friends that borders on the mysterious, I find the conversation always end in a stalemate. I've learned that, as with religion and politics, it's best to avoid such controversial subjects. But, of course, this is not always possible. I once found myself in such a situation when, out of the blue, I had to answer some questions arising from newspaper reports about Southeast Asia's *"yeti,"* the legendary Big Foot. After that, all people had to do was hear my name and they would say: "You don't really believe in that, do you?" I finally gave up trying to defend myself and avoided the Big Foot subject altogether.

I don't want to confirm or deny that I believe in Big Foot, but what I would like to do is report what I have uncovered, and what happened to me in the Malay jungle a number of years ago, and then let you, the reader, be the judge. I will admit that I would not be retelling my experiences with Big Foot had not the Chinese recently revealed the results of research on the subject they have been conducting over the years. The Chinese are less skeptical, and treat the subject with all seriousness. In fact, they have set up a government agency to investigate this rather interesting phenomenon.

With me it began in the spring of 1970 when I was invited by Tunku Bakar, a Malay prince from Johor State, to join him and some friends on a fishing trip on the Endau River in Malaysia. Among those invited were an interesting group of jungle-bashers, including Kurt Rolfes, an ex-combat

The author, left, poses with fish he caught on the Endau River in Malaysia. Photo by Kurt Rolfes. Right, the author (hat) with Chief Game Warden (far left) on the Libir River in the Malay jungle. Photo by Mike Yamashita

photographer in Vietnam. When they spoke about wild elephants and tigers and primitive orang asli, I quickly accepted the invitation. Aside from fishing, there was always the possibility that the trip might offer some unexpected excitement. You never quite know what will happen on the Endau.

The unexpected excitement in this case turned out to be the monsoon rains that came early that year. Instead of finding good fishing, a fast-rising river forced us to seek shelter in an orang asli village. For three wet, uncomfortable days we sat on mats in a bamboo house built on stilts, and, while smoke filtered up between cracks in the floor to keep mosquitoes at bay, we listened to Prince Bakar translate orang asli tales of the jungles.

The stories, which seemed to be based mostly on native superstition, revealed how the white-handed gibbon's hands became white, why the tongue of a certain lizard is red, and other such unhelpful bits of information. They had jungle yarns to tell, too, about rogue elephants, man-eating tigers and giant catfish that weigh 300 pounds. Then casually the headman said: "We saw the footprints again."

"What footprints?"

"The giant people, orang dalam."

"Where did you see them?" I asked, half-heartedly. No doubt I was going to hear about another local superstition.

"Far upriver," the man replied, earnestly. "Above the twelfth rapid beyond the Kimchin. Orang dalam live on the high plateau and come down to the river when it's dry."

At the time I didn't put much faith in what the old man was telling me. I knew that these jungle folk, people who are not far removed from the Stone Age, had no shortage of myths and folklore, combined perhaps with an active imagination. But it made good listening and did help pass the time.

Once back in Singapore I would most likely have forgotten about Big Foot and jungle giants had it not been for my Chinese friend, Tan Khia Fatt. We were having lunch a few days after I returned and he was anxious to hear about

186

my trip. He chuckled about the orang asli, until I mentioned Big Foot. The expression on his face suddenly changed.

"It's more than native talk," he said, in the tone a teacher uses when scolding a pupil.

"You don't believe in these giants?" I said jokingly.

He didn't answer immediately. He was forming his thoughts to make his words convincing. "During the Malay National Emergency," he began slowly, "when the Chinese terrorists roamed the jungle freely, there were many reports of strange jungle people. It was all in the newspapers."

"But that doesn't make it true, just because it's in the newspapers," I said.

"OK, but I happened to be there," he snapped. He waited for me to say something, but I said nothing. "It was in Johor," he began. "On the road between Mersing and JB. I was a young insurance salesman and had to do a lot of traveling in Malaysia. I had an old car and did most of my driving at night. It was a wild stretch of road I was on that night when suddenly I saw two cars stopped in front of me. At first I thought they were in an accident, but when I jumped out I found that the driver and his passenger in the lead car were in a kind of shock."

Khia Fatt stopped to compose himself, and began again.

"They said they had been speeding along when suddenly a hairy creature, like an ape but walking upright, came out of the forest and started across the road. They had to skid to a stop to avoid hitting him. The creature stopped when he heard the brakes and saw the lights. He paused, and then returned in the same direction from which he had come. The driver in the second car saw him too, just as he was entering the jungle."

Khia Fatt described in more detail what the two drivers had seen, and concluded by saying that the story appeared in *The Straits Times* the next day.

Maybe the headman on the Endau was right.

It wasn't long after my meeting with Khia Fatt that I began to do my homework at the National Library. I read through rolls of microfilm of *The Straits Times* and old magazines. It was slow work. The National Emergency covered a span of years. I was about to give up when I reached the fall of 1953. Then I saw it. The black print seemed to leap out at me.

It was Christmas Day. A young Chinese woman named Wong Yee Moi was tapping rubber trees on an estate in south Perak, when she felt a hand on her shoulder and turned to be "confronted by the most revolting female" one could possibly imagine. This she-thing was covered with hair, had white Caucasoid-type skin and long black hair. She wore a loin cloth of bark and stank as if "of an animal."

The female grinned and revealed long nasty fangs. Yee Moi fled in panic for the compound, but not before sighting two similar types she thought to be males, standing in the shade of trees by the river. They had mustaches hanging down to their waists.

The estate manager, a Scot named Browne, immediately called the National Security Force's local headquarters which responded immediately with a posse of Malay security guards. On searching the estate, the guards spotted three hairy types on the river bank—such as described by Yee Moi. The creatures dived underwater, emerged on the far bank and vanished into the jungle.

Had only one person, and a panic-stricken one at that, made a report to the authorities that she had seen and been accosted by three hairy jungle creatures, we might easily dismiss the story as being fiction. But when the security guards saw the same creatures, it had to be something more than a thing imagined.

Nor did the incident end there. The following day, a Hindu worker was squatting to tap a flow of rubber latex when he was encircled by a pair of hairy arms. In a rage of fear, he broke loose only to fall into a dead faint on his way back to the compound. He revived to find the same trio standing over him, laughing at his discomfiture.

Again we could say that the unfortunate Hindu laborer was frightened by the story Yee Moi had told and had imagined seeing these creatures. But when the security guards were summoned, they too saw the same hairy creatures on the riverbank. Newspapers and Radio Malaya reported the sightings and brought forth official statements from such sources as the Department of Museums and Aboriginal Research. Authorities believed that this could be "one of the most valuable anthropological discoveries since Darwin."

Official reports also disclosed that this wasn't the first time such sightings in Malaya had been recorded. I had to dig deeper, into dusty old volumes in the basement at the National Library in Singapore. Again, I hit pay dirt. Two British anthropologists, Skeat and Blagden, wrote in *The Pagan Races of the Malay Peninsula* that orang asli encountered such jungle types, which they called *orang dalam,* or translated—'interior people.' According to the two men, these people lived in high remote cloud forests, and were large and hairy. They were sometimes referred to as 'the stinking ones.' It was more than just a coincidence that the headman on the Endau had also spoken of them as 'interior people.'

The sketch on the left, property of the American Museum of Natural History, was made by an English explorer over a 100 years ago. At right, pushing a dugout over rapids on Endau River in search of the Asian Big Foot.

189

Other reports of hairy jungle people went back even further. In 1871, an Englishman, A.D. Frederickson, wrote the following about his travels in Malaya: "A curious specimen of a hairy humanity, not unlike Darwin's idea of the origin of the species, was at the time of my visit being conveyed to the coast for shipment to some society in Calcutta. This is the individual as he appeared." A sketch of the creature was included with the report, which is now the property of the American Museum of Natural History.

In Southeast Asia, there was certainly evidence documenting the existence of hairy jungle creatures that inhabit the Malay Peninsula, but did it have any direct relationship with what the natives on the Endau River had indicated to me? Did they actually see such tracks as they described to me, only a week or two before I arrived at their settlement?

Detailed maps of the Malay jungles are restricted, but I was fortunate to be able to get a copy of the Endau region at British Army Headquarters. I studied the river in detail. I located the village where we stayed and followed the river up to the rapids. I counted them—twelve. The headman said there were twelve rapids that led to the Kimchin. But beyond that the area was marked 'relief data incomplete.'

Why incomplete?

"Quite simple to explain," the British officer said. "It's due to clouds. The maps are compiled from aerial photographs. This is a high region. Most likely some kind of plateau."

Again it was more than coincidence. The headman had said there were twelve rapids and a plateau. His people must have been there—at least to the foot of the plateau, near the headwaters of the Endau. Also, Skeat and Blagden made mention of 'cloud forests.' Other things began to fall into place. For example, every report I had read about the hairy creatures revealed they had a foul odor about them. The headman told me the same, that Big Foot smelled terribly.

I had gone as far as I could with the research. There was

only one way left to see if there was any truth in what I had read and heard, and that was to organize an expedition and go into the jungle.

Forming an expedition is not that easy. You do not simply announce that you are going into the jungle to look for the legendary Big Foot. If you do, you're immediately accused of seeking publicity, looking for the sensational. There is another reason for wanting to be anonymous. Big Foot is an extremely sensitive subject in most Asian countries. Government officials shun such publicity. It's best to avoid mentioning Big Foot altogether. I had to keep the expedition quiet. If we found something, it might be different.

The jungle I wanted to visit was unexplored, and at that time I did not know game warden Mohammed Khan or anyone in the Game Department. I would have to make the arrangements on my own. To succeed, the expedition would have to be well planned and well equipped. The river could be treacherous, with uncertain rapids, snakes and crocodiles. For certain, the jungle teamed with elephants and tigers. There was even a rumor that a man-eating tiger had just taken its 26th victim. Nor could we expect much outside help once we passed beyond the first rapids. There were no more aboriginal settlements, and what lay at the headwaters of the Endau, even the orang asli didn't know. Nevertheless, I still wanted to give it a try.

I was fortunate that Kurt Rolfes, an ex-combat photographer from Vietnam, was as interested in Big Foot as I was. We decided to set up an expedition together. Kurt had his own photo studio in Singapore and could spare the time. For the next year we planned the expedition. From Wildlife Safaris in Singapore we were able to get most of the necessary equipment and the much needed help of an experienced jungle hand who knew the Malay jungle well. He was an Eurasian, Kenny Nelson. Kenny was keen on making the trip. As far back as he could remember, he had wanted to explore the headwaters of the Endau. He also knew two orang asli, Bojung and Achin, who lived at the settlement and who were willing to serve as porters.

Further help came from Captain Patrick Coverton of the Second King Edward VII's Own Gurkha Rifles. Captain Coverton was instructor in the Jungle Warfare School at Kota Tinggi and had a Gurkha company under his command. He regretted he couldn't make the entire trip with us, but he would see us part of the way up the river, at least to the first rapids.

Captain Coverton made good his promise to me. We camped with him and his Gurkhas along the bank of the lower Endau, and several days later met Kenny and the orang asli porters at the first rapids.

Kenny had some bad news. When we planned the expedition, our friend Prince Bakar intended to join us. As the nephew of the Sultan of Johor, he would have no difficulty in getting help to us if we got into difficulties. He was also going to bring arms. Kenny now explained that Bakar was laid up in hospital.

We couldn't turn back at this point. With or without Bakar's help, we decided to continue.

Our 16-foot-long boat, when fully loaded, was but inches above water. We had a six-horsepower outboard to take us part of the way up the river to shallow water. After that we would all take turns at the paddles. Captain Coverton and his Gurkhas accompanied us to the rapids and there we bade our good-byes. Five of us—the two orang asli porters, Kenny Nelson, Kurt and I—set out, and just as we were about to go around a bend further upriver, I looked back. Captain Coverton was still standing where we had left him, waiting for us to disappear into the jungle. He had wanted desperately to join us but his higher command would not authorize a search for a legendary jungle giant.

Four miles farther upriver we came to our second set of rapids. The fun part of the trip was over. Everything had to be unloaded and carried over slippery rocks to the river above. Then came the grueling task of pushing and pulling the boat up the swirling falls, inch by inch. It was impossible for us to keep dry.

The lower Endau is wide and muddy, and swampy along the banks. Here crocodiles lurk among the reeds. Above the rapids there are fewer mud banks and very few crocodiles, so we could swim with reasonable safety. Often we pushed the boat along using it only to carry our supplies. At best, we could do ten or eleven miles a day.

The deeper we penetrated, the more beautiful the jungle became. The forest was triple canopy with trees and trailing vines hundreds of feet high. Unseen birds sang from the treetops and playful monkeys dropped from dizzy heights to the branches below. The jungle was pristine, almost pure. We hated to talk, or even leave a footprint on a bank for fear of changing it all.

Kurt and I, however, did want to walk the banks whenever possible. We were checking tracks, our prime purpose, but where the banks ended, we found it best to swim the river or walk with water up to our armpits rather than hack through the jungle. The jungle was dark and uncertain, and in many places so dense we could hardly pass without chopping through. Then when we began cutting a path, leeches fell upon us like raindrops. If we didn't stop on the spot to burn them off with a cigarette, and merely tried to flick them away, they left nasty wounds which began to fester a few days later. Survival means puffing on a cigar or cheroot all day long. It was best to chance the river.

The banks were now a maze of tracks—deer, pig, turtle, monitor lizard, elephant, tiger, leopard, tapir. The tapir we thought, at first, were rhino. Tiger tracks were the most frequent.

We passed beyond the tributary of the Kimchin and continued up the Endau. A few days later we reached the twelfth rapid above the Kimchin. Just before dark we found a wide sand bank, a good place to set up camp. While Bojung and Achin were busy with the lean-to and gathering firewood,

Kurt and I crossed the river to the other bank to look for tracks. All along the sand bank were elephant tracks with fresh droppings, and numerous tiger tracks.

Kurt was in the lead, stopping often to check each track carefully. Suddenly he stopped. He spread out his arms, a signal for me to stop. He stood motionless, staring down at the crusted sand. For a long time he didn't move, as though he was mesmerized by something he saw. You often hear about snakes in the jungle, especially cobras, that can cause a person or an animal to freeze. For a moment I thought this might be what Kurt had encountered, a coiled cobra blocking his path. But I quickly realized snakes didn't come out into the hot sun. It had to be something else. I cautiously moved up to where Kurt stood. Still he did not say anything, nor did he turn to face me. But he knew I was there, and he pointed down to the sand for me to see. There in front of us were footprints, human footprints, though not ordinary ones. They were enormous, 19 inches long and 10 inches wide. The creature that had made them had come down from the jungle and entered the water and here the tracks disappeared.

We called the others. Bojung, followed by Achin, came half running and half swimming across the river. They stopped dead. Bojung shook his head. "Orang dalam," he said. They insisted we go back to camp with them, which we did, but not before Kurt photographed the tracks.

It was a tense evening. Judging by all the tracks, the river where we were camped was the junction of a game trail: elephant, tiger and the questionable human tracks. But what kind of human tracks? Achin refused to talk about it. And when we finally cajoled Bojung to loosen up and speak, Achin withdrew to the far end of the lean-to and covered his head, so as not to hear our conversation.

Because we were skeptical, Bojung became positive. We knew orang asli were honest people. They are superstitious but they don't deliberately tell lies. What Bojung had to tell us, he swore, on the head of his newborn son, was true.

The year before, it was Bojung who had been with the headman when they saw the tracks of the man-beast orang dalam. Neither of them actually saw the creature, but others from their village did, including the headman's father. What was so amazing about the story that Bojung had to tell was that it confirmed things I had heard and read about in my research about the giants.

The size of the man-beast varies. He is described as being anything from six to nine feet tall. All agree that he is hairy but not furry. Males have much hair about their head, chest, arms and legs. Their eyes are red, or at least bloodshot. And all reports claim they give off a powerful odor which Bojung likened to 'monkey urine.'

Another interesting characteristic about the creatures is that, at first contact, they appear to be friendly. They usually make the overtures and approach slowly. Then, for some reason, they become frightened and flee into the jungle.

The question that comes to mind is how do such creatures evade detection from man? I found this most baffling, but the orang asli didn't. Bojung pointed out that elephants and

Stephens, with Bojung looking on, points to huge footprints in the sand along a river bank in a remote area of the Malay jungle. Photo by Kurt Rolfes.

buffalo flee from the approach of man. Even a large herd of elephants can vanish unheard and undetected into the jungle, yet their footprints are still filling with water as men approach. Why then can't a creature—perhaps a sub-human with a higher degree of intelligence than the average animal—cunningly and cleverly keep clear of man?

Furthermore, how well explored is the jungle? Man may paddle up a river or walk along a game trail, but what does he know about what actually lies beyond that riverbank or beyond the edge of the trail? He sees little, like one who walks down Singapore's Orchard Road, stares at the buildings and then claims to know what goes on behind their closed doors.

Skeptics are fond of saying that in this day and age there cannot possibly be any group or race of people or animal alive which is unknown to science. But every year new species of animals are discovered, and nearly every decade or so tribes or races that have previously been regarded as purely legendary or mythical are encountered by unimpeachable witnesses. Was it not only a few years ago that a Stone Age tribe was discovered in the Philippines?

The Himalayan yeti, or the Abominable Snowman, is the subject of stories that never die, and there will always be both doubters and believers. But the search for Big Foot doesn't stop in Asia. According to Peter Byrne, who founded the Intentional Wildlife Organization Society, the Asian Big Foot may have crossed over the land mass between the eastern and western hemispheres "thousands of years ago, probably around 500 AD or so, and still exists in isolated remote spots in the northwest, Canada and Alaska." In America it's called Sasquatch, Indian for Big Foot.

People have been sighting Big Foot or finding his prints in the wilderness of the vast Pacific Northwest ever since the white man first went into that part of the world. There are more than a thousand reports of sightings, and casts of footprints abound. In 1967, near Bluff Creek in northern California, Roger Patterson was knocked from his startled horse by a creature that looked more human than animal. Patterson was able to click off six feet of movie film. When it was developed it caused a worldwide stir. From the left of the screen, the creature walked on two feet in long smooth strides. She (with plainly visible breasts) crossed a dried riverbed covered with rocks and dead wood. The creature was large, perhaps seven feet tall and three feet broad. She swung her arms almost like a human. She stared straight at the camera, paused, turned and then walked away into the forest.

Could it be fake? Film technicians say the cost of such an accomplished fraud would be enormous, and certainly beyond the range of Patterson's income. John Napier, formerly director of the Smithsonian Institute of Washington, DC, admitted he could see "no way that the film is a hoax."

There are skeptics who ask if it could have been a man in a gorilla suit. I was fortunate to have seen the film, run at normal speed and again in slow motion. When Kurt and I had our Endau River film developed and stories of our find appeared in America, I was asked to attend a symposium in New York. The Big Foot shots Kurt took were projected on a wall-size screen and many scientists in the field studied them and asked questions. They then showed me the movie film. As this creature slowly walked away I could plainly see the back muscles in motion—which could never happen in someone were wearing a gorilla suit. Peter Byrne also ruled it out. No one could ever fake the height and huge stride, nor would they risk being shot.

There may be skeptics, but, nevertheless, Washington state has imposed a $10,000 fine for "the wanton slaying of the ape-creature." Maybe state officials should reconsider and make it voluntary manslaughter. Who knows?

Big Foot runs the risk of being shot without provocation. Anything man doesn't understand he shoots. The security guards in Malaysia opened fire on the man-beasts when they would not respond to their shouts. I read of another account that took place in Burma before World War II. A hunter sighted down his gun barrel what appeared to be "an ape with human traits." He pulled the trigger and struck the beast in the chest. It let out a most pitiful scream, whereupon a much larger animal, evidently the mother, rushed from the forest, picked up the wounded child in her arms and dashed for cover.

Some remarkable Big Foot stories have come out of China since that country opened her doors a few years ago. In fact, stories about wild men in China go back 3000 years. A chronicle of the Warring States Period (476-221 BC), relates how a captured wild man was presented as a gift to the king of the eastern Zhou dynasty several centuries earlier.

Newspaper articles published in Beijing have quoted 17th century records as saying: "In the remote mountains of Fang Xian country, there are rock caves in which live hairy men as tall as three meters." That's nine feet tall.

More than 300 sightings of wild men have been recorded there since the 1920s. Four scientific expeditions have searched for the wild man since 1976. They penetrated the mountainous, thickly forested Shen Nong Jia region of northwestern Hu Bei, where reports have been most persistent. In 1980, Meng Qing Bao, leader of one expedition, found more than 1000 footprints stretching for about one-and-a-half miles. The team made a plaster cast of the most prominent print, which was more than 20 inches long and showed the largest of the five toes splayed outwards.

In recent years there have been so many sightings that in 1981 the Chinese set up a bureau called the Society for the Survey and Research of the Chinese Wild Man. Its Secretary General is Li Jian, a 65-year-old historian and director of the prominent Historical Research Institute of China's Provincial Academy of Sciences. The society's 400 members include scientists, teachers and government officials.

Li says China's wild man, which they call *ye ren,* looks rather different from Big Foot as reported in the West: "What is special about this beast is that it walks like a human being, has no tail but has hair all over its body." According to Li, *ye ren* is about six feet tall, has the ability to laugh, can weave bamboo and enjoys the warmth of a fire. Most sightings have been noted in the Shen Nong Jia region, a rugged area of high mountains and deep valleys with heavy vegetation and caves.

The society gives credence to sightings that are at close range, last longer than a glimpse and are reported by several people, preferably officials or scientists.

During a three-hour meeting in the Hu Bei provincial capital of Wu Han, Li discussed the evidence collected. "A wild man is so powerful he can bend pieces of bamboo," he said. "He must also have hands able to twist bamboo. Only humans have such hands, but we don't have the power to do it."

Li gave a case example of a recent sighting. In a small town in southern China near the Burmese border, a schoolteacher heard the village dogs barking. Thinking a wild animal was prowling near his house, Li Ming Zhi took his hunting rifle and stepped outside. In the moonlight he saw another villager and walked up to greet him. To his horror, he found himself face to face not with a human being but with a giant hairy primate. For five minutes they stared at each other, Li not daring to touch or shoot the creature which later disappeared into the dense forest. The incident might have been dismissed as a figment of Li's imagination had there not been dozens of others who also saw the creature.

Some peasants, Li Jian claims, have grappled with wild men. In September 1979, a cowherder in Fang Xian province said a wild man gripped his wrist and held him for half an hour, laughing all the while. When the cowherder broke free and ran home, there were finger-shaped blue bruises on his wrists.

The Chinese press, which periodically speculates about wild men, related how a hunter caught a young wild man in a trap in 1980. The hunter told a reporter that the creature's eyes were filled with tears. Being superstitious, the hunter thought it was the reincarnation of a dead companion and let it go.

Li said he thought the wild man was "linked more closely to human beings" than to apes or monkeys. "Apes cannot walk long distances. In addition, the wild man is more intelligent than apes," he said.

There were theories, he said, of the wild men being the survivors of a species of giant apes thought to be extinct. He himself became interested in the phenomenon in the early 1970s but he admitted there is deep skepticism in China as to whether or not the wild man exists. But he told the story of a skeptical party secretary who openly declared he did not believe in wild men. His reason was that he had never seen one. Sometime later the party secretary called Li to say he had changed his mind. While driving in a car with five companions, they had seen a wild man framed in the headlights and had actually got out of the car to look at it before it fled into the woods. Li admitted that he had yet to see a wild man himself, though he encountered footprints on one expedition.

"I believe the wild man exists," he said. "It is only a matter of time before we prove it."

In Guandong there is a permanent exhibition on display for the hunt for the legendary "Abominable Snowman." *The Yangcheng Evening News* reported that Mr. Fang Zhong Shi, head of the China Wild Man Research Association, has a standing offer of a 10,000 yuan (about US$10,000) reward through the paper for anyone bringing in one of the wild creatures.

The question still remains. Does an Asian version of Big Foot exist? I am not convinced, but my own search has not ended on the Endau or any other river in Asia. I can say it began on the Endau. There are other rivers, and other jungles. Maybe a few years from now it won't be so strange. For more than 300 years there was talk of an ape-like man living in darkest Africa. A hundred years ago, the first gorilla was found and the myth ended.

As amazing as the jungles of Southeast Asia are, they are no less so than the primitive people who live there. Take the jungles of southern Thailand and Malaysia. The aborigines, or orang asli, who live in these dark forests are divided into three groups: Negritos, Senoi and Proto-Malays. Sometimes we hear the name Sakai, another Malay word for Senoi, and Proto-Malays may be called "aboriginal Malays." However, whatever the name used, together they are called orang asli, a name they prefer. Loosely translated it means "original man."

Negritos are anthropologically Southeast Asia's oldest existing race. They are nomadic and move about in groups, seldom more than a dozen in close families.

Their life is simple. They have no shelter, except during monsoons when they throw leaves over poles to ward off the rain. They are basically hunters and collectors of forest produce. Some do plant small patches of crops such as tapioca and bananas.

Negrito skin color is dark chocolate brown, but no darker. In remote forests, men wear pieces of twisted bark cloth around their waists, while women weave grass and leaves to make skirts. Negritos who live close to advanced communities have adopted Western garb. Men wear shorts, and women dress in sarongs. Both wear rubber sandals.

With blowpipes and poison darts, men hunt for squirrels, monkeys, rats, lizards and birds. Women and children gather fruit and vegetables from the forest. Fish are caught in traps or speared with sharpened bamboo. Sometimes tuba, a strong form of tranquilizer, is used to stun the fish and bring them to the surface.

Senoi are slightly taller than Negritos and have a somewhat slimmer build. Their skin color is medium brown, and they have the characteristics of the Chinese.

Some Senoi paint their faces and themselves. Others pierce their noses and insert decorated pieces of wood and bone or porcupine quills. Most of the Sanoi groups practice shifting cultivation of some kind, often combining it with permanent types of agriculture such as rubber growing and rice cultivation.

There are estimated to be some 60,000 Senoi. They build

semi-permanent type dwellings near their fields. These are attap-covered huts, built on stilts. The walls and floors are split bamboo. Hearths for fire are made of hard-packed earth in wooden frames.

Proto-Malays, or aboriginal Malays, are heavier built than the other two groups. They are by far the most advanced and many have been assimilated into Malay society. They find employment as policemen, laborers, boat repairers and fishermen. Their homes and dwellings are similar to the Malays. Some Proto-Malays are sea people who live aboard their boats. They number about 30,000.

Often when I tell people about the Oriental jungle, they look at me with skepticism. They refuse to believe that here in crowded Asia, and not too many miles north of busy Singapore, there is a huge, wild, untamed jungle, parts of which remain unexplored to this very day. Nor do they quite believe it has tigers and elephants and pythons and small dark people who call themselves orang asli—the Original Man.

People find it most difficult to comprehend that some of these jungle people have never seen other human beings, except for members of their own tribe, and that civilization, with its shiny beads and brightly colored cloth, cannot tempt them to give up their jungle ways. When I want to win my point, I tell people about Muda, whom you met briefly in Chapter 2. I tell them that this strange little jungle man was the soul of the Malaysian jungle; then one day he died.

The death of this jungle man upset me deeply. I try to rationalize his death, that he, like his father, and his father's father, for more than 10,000 years of jungle survival, have each, in turn, had to pass from life into the uncertainty we call death. Each had lived and died. But such thoughts are not comforting. I didn't know them, but I did know Muda. He was my teacher. He taught me something about life.

I first met Muda on one of my earlier trips into the Malay jungles with game warden Mohammed Khan. I had rendezvoused with Mohammed at Tembling Halt from where we took government river boats for the three-hour trip up the Tembling to the National Park headquarters. That first evening at the headquarters was exhilarating, meeting the rangers and guides, and listening to their talk about wild elephants, tigers, seladeng and other strange creatures we would have the chance to meet in the next three weeks. The subject then turned to the area into which we were going.

It was an unknown country.

"You'll need a porter," Mohammed said to me and called for a Negrito who had shown up at the park a few days before.

We were discussing our plans when the man appeared, following a few steps behind a ranger. He was clad in baggy shorts, no doubt rejects given him to replace a breech cloth. The only other thing he wore was a black band made of bark tightly bound above his right biceps. They had given him the name Muda.

Muda never once raised his eyes. He was 40, maybe 45. He could have been younger, or older. He was painfully shy, and even after agreeing to carry my supplies, he did not look up.

The next morning we set out and by evening we had traveled as far upriver as the longboats could go. The boats returned, leaving as alone in the jungle. There was but one way to go now—to the unexplored central basin to locate the source of the Lebir River. When we found the source, we would build rafts and float down river to civilization on the east coast of the peninsula.

Muda and the other Negritoes each carried staggering loads of 90 pounds. At first, I must admit, I was annoyed with Muda. I had bought in the US a new pack for the trip, with padded shoulder straps and a back support that the Swiss manufacturers guaranteed was the latest in camping technology. When I turned the pack over to Muda, he slipped it into a basket he had fashioned from rattan and which he supported by a thin bark head strap. If he wanted to be uncomfortable, who was I to argue with him?

When we entered the jungle a change came over Muda. He assumed a position of responsibility which no one was likely to challenge. We were astonished at his ability to maneuver in the jungle. Our first encounter after leaving the river was to scale a steep bank which was slippery and muddy with only thin roots for support. Muda went up with the ease of someone riding an escalator. He took the lead, swinging his knife with such precision he could make a branch fall in any direction he willed.

The first few days in the jungle are always the worst. Everything seems magnified. Each shadow lurks with some terrifying, unseen demon. Each overhead branch holds a slimy creature ready to drop. Each turn brings you face-to-face with some frightful jungle beast. But Muda was there to give a helping hand. In the beginning, he never let me out of his sight.

But we soon became adjusted to our environment and the surroundings, and Muda turned to other things. He scampered up incredibly high trees to bring down ripe jungle fruit, and when the group called a break he rushed ahead to scout out a trail to save us unnecessary steps.

He never seemed to tire. He banked the fire in the evening after everyone turned in, and he was the first to rise in the morning to start the fire and put the pot on for tea. The more I watched him, the more curious I became. Why was he leading us? Who was he? What were his thoughts about intruders like us in his jungle? I had to find the answers. Maybe when we sat around the campfire in the evenings.

Those evenings, after tired bodies had bathed in the river and darkness had closed in, were always delightful. There's something very private about the jungle at night. The world becomes just a sphere that encompasses the circle of light around the campfire. The light is like a cage, not sealing you in but closing the jungle out.

Around the warming fire, backs against the forest, everyone sat. Rangers translated the tales the Negritoes had to tell. They were wild and exaggerated stories that baffled the imagination. They took turns. One scout told how a rogue elephant had destroyed his camp. Another talked about a python that swallowed an infant. Then it was Muda's turn. He was walking along a river bank when he became aware that a tiger was following him. He knew that to turn and face him with a spear was certain death. To run would have been equally bad. So he used psychology, only he didn't call it that. He let the tiger know he, Muda, was aware that he, the tiger, was there. Why does he not run, the tiger thought. Maybe he wants me to attack! The tiger became uncertain, and went his own way into the jungle.

Through a ranger I talked to Muda and asked him his rightful name, not his given name.

"Muda," he said. "Why do I need another name?"

He was right. Why did he need another name? "Okay, how old are you?" I asked. He didn't know.

"Are you married?" He lived with women, yes.

"Do you have children?" He had to count. "Yes, four."

"How old are they?" He didn't know. The concept of time or age had no meaning for him. He quickly became bored with the conversation.

In later conversations I had to avoid anything to do with time. A day to him was understandable because it had a beginning and an end. But what was a year when there are no seasons? Or even a day, when it was like every other day? Life simply moved on. As with his father, and his father's father, Muda lived in a timeless environment. His history was his memory, his present what he could see and hear around him, his future what was beyond the next bend in the river.

There were other things we learned from Muda. Jungle knowledge. He pointed out fruit and wild berries we could eat. He showed us game trails and knew almost to the hour when game had last passed. Every turned leaf, every bent twig, every disturbed vine had a meaning. They were unwritten signs in his jungle that were as clear as traffic signs in our city streets. And like city signs they, too, had to be observed.

Certain leaves we couldn't touch, certain mud holes we couldn't cross, certain short cuts we had to avoid.

After a week of hacking through the jungle, or following game trails where we could, we reached the Lebir River. Now came the task of building rafts. I worked with Muda. We felled bamboos, some 30 feet in length. These we dragged to the river, where Muda showed me how to lash them together with strips of rattan. Each raft contained exactly nine bamboo logs and measured about six feet wide. At the very center we constructed a raised platform for our gear. Each man cut his own twelve-foot-long pole.

We shoved off, using the poles to avoid rocks and great trees floating down river. Our rafts moved among the strange wreckage of the jungle in the slow motion of the current. The sun revolved around us. The great impenetrable walls of the jungle rose up on both sides of the river. And always standing on the bow, with his long pole in hand, was Muda, listening and reading the signs.

One afternoon as we were drifting thus, down river, each man lost in his own thoughts, Muda, his eyes straight ahead, spoke out in a loud voice to the jungle. Who was he talking to? There was nothing but the green monotony of the foliage. Presently a voice came back, faint in the distance.

"Who is it?" I whispered to Muda.

He turned to face me and, tapping upon his chest, proudly said: "Orang asli." How profound were his two words! Here, indeed, was original man.

We never saw the Negrito with whom he spoke; the voice remained as mysterious as the jungle itself. But we did meet others of his kind, almost always by accident. We drifted around one bend and there was a Negrito man and his woman. She cradled a small child. His only clothing was a breech cloth. She was naked. They were traveling upriver on a three-log bamboo raft loaded with ripe durians.

We tried to barter for their durians. What did they want? Rice, coffee, dried fish? They wanted nothing. They gave us their durians. "We just can't take their food from them," I said to Mohammed and reached into my pocket. I pulled out a five-dollar Malaysian note. Mohammed laughed.

"He doesn't even have a pocket to put it into," he said. The game warden was right, and what could the jungle man possibly do with money? I stuffed the note back into my pocket and we went on.

I couldn't help wondering what would happen if these Negritoes were exposed to civilization: would they accept it? Is not human nature the same the world over? That night I was anxious to discuss this with Mohammed. I waited until we were seated around the campfire.

"Civilization does not interest them," Mohammed explained.

"But what if you introduce them to luxuries?" I asked.

"It means nothing to them."

I disagreed with Mohammed. Negritoes were no different from anyone else. The truth I was soon to learn.

After ten days on the river, we came to a grass house, a few more miles, and more houses, finally a settlement, and then a town.

Aboard our bamboo rafts, using poles to avoid rocks, we floated down river among the strange wreckage of the jungle, in the slow motion of the current.

Generally, in the jungle, we set up camp early in the afternoon. But on the last day we were anxious to reach a bridge that spanned the river. It was the railway line running north into Kelantan. It was dark when we reached the bridge. We abandoned our rafts and scampered up the bank and waited on the tracks for the northbound train.

Our Negritoes had never seen tracks, nor a locomotive, nor, for that matter, vehicles, electricity or telephones. In fact, the only buildings they had seen were those at park headquarters. And now in the night we were waiting for a train to arrive. Muda stood, staring at the tracks that reached out into the empty night, waiting, saying nothing.

Presently the train came, thundering up the tracks, belching out steam. The solitary light at first appeared like a pin-hole on a black screen, growing brighter and brighter, until it was blinding. Still Muda said nothing. Mohammed flagged down the train.

We were a motley band filing aboard, clad in jungle gear, carrying packs, with three Negritoes and their rattan baskets and head straps. Passengers did a double take.

The calmness of the Negritoes baffled me. I asked a ranger to find out from Muda his thoughts. His reply was straightforward. "I led you through the jungle and you trusted me. Now I follow you and I trust you." He sincerely believed we would let no harm befall him.

We disembarked at the next town. It was nearly midnight. We had to find rooms. We located a small Chinese hotel and awoke the proprietor. He flicked on a light and slid open the iron gate, only to slam it shut again.

"No rooms. We're full," he said when he saw us.

I tried the next hotel, while everyone waited down the street. The Chinese keeper smiled when he saw a lone foreigner. "Five rooms. Ten of us," I explained. "We're on a fishing trip. You know, fishing."

He nodded and I signed the register.

The poor man could not believe what he saw entering his

hotel, but there was nothing he could do about it now. I don't think he slept for the two nights we were there.

Muda and a young Negrito boy moved into my room. At first they stumbled along, pushing one another into the lead. It was all bewildering and a little frightening, as though they were stepping into a tiger's cage and didn't know where the tiger was.

After a few minutes curiosity got the better of them. Door knobs fascinated them, light switches startled them, mirrors brought out their best smiles. But most bewildering were the flushing toilets. A pull of a chain and water mysteriously came gushing seemingly from nowhere. It was magic.

Finally, after convincing them we must sleep, the boy curled up on the rug on the floor and Muda took priority on the other bed. He rolled himself up in the sheet until only his nose stuck out from one corner. Sometimes in the night I was dimly aware of water flushing and doors opening and closing, but I was too tired to care.

At dawn I awoke, conscious of eyes staring at me. Muda was squatting on the other bed waiting for me to awake. The boy was sitting on the dresser. Beyond our door was a world to discover.

We were hungry, but it was obvious our attire would not be acceptable in a restaurant or anywhere around town. I agreed to meet Mohammed and the others at a small restaurant, but first I would buy the Negritoes some simple clothing. We headed for the first Chinese shop we could find.

A Chinese girl waited on us, unsmiling and not too keen about serving three "savages" who were getting into all the shelves and drawers. It was difficult to control them. "Only what we need," I tried to explain to them, a kind of rule of the jungle they managed to understand. They chose one sports shirt and one pair of shorts each. The shirts were flaming colors, and the shorts were several sizes too large. For myself, I picked out a bottle of shampoo and after shave lotion. They each picked out a bottle of shampoo and after shave lotion.

This was too much. Negritoes have little hair and no whiskers. "You don't need these," I snapped and took the bottles away from them. Muda looked at me with sad eyes. My mind flashed back to the jungles. When Muda climbed a dangerously high tree and brought down ripe rambutans, he didn't tell me I didn't need any to eat. Nor did he keep the fish he caught for himself. The jungle gave him what he wanted, and he shared that with me. Civilization gave me what I wanted, so why shouldn't I share with him? They got their shampoo and after shave lotion. We added three new pairs of white sneakers to the list. I was careful not to try on socks.

Out in the street they looked like real dandies, walking in their white shoes in duck-like steps. I had to keep them in line, or they would be run down by cars and motorbikes. And I was forever stopping, kneeling down and tying their shoelaces. For some reason they couldn't master the knots.

Then came their first meal, sitting at a table, with knives and forks, plates and cups and all the uncomfortable refinements of "civilization." Mohammed and the rangers were waiting when we arrived.

Mohammed ordered and thought it best that their food be placed on individual plates before them, rather than communal dining. It was fine with our friends. They began eating from one end of their plates and worked across to the other. I offered Muda some salt. He took a handful and gulped it down. For a treat we bought ice cream with our coffee. They had never tasted anything cold before. Muda solved the problem by dropping his ice cream into his cup of coffee.

That night we took them to the town's only movie, a Chinese *kung fu* film. They ducked when swords were swung; they marveled when heroes leaped over buildings; they shouted threats of warning at the villains when they appeared. They saw the film at least six times in the next two days.

On the third morning, government Land Rovers were coming to pick us up. Rangers explained to Muda that he and the other Negritoes would be taken back to park headquarters, where they had started. It would be a long trip lasting several days. I would not be traveling with them.

I awoke at dawn that morning, strangely aware that something was wrong. I sat up with a start. Muda and the boy were not in the room. What trouble were they in now? I quickly slipped on my trousers and dashed for the door. I opened it and almost tripped, for there on the doorstep were two pairs of shoes, the laces tied in bows, and beneath the shoes were shorts and shirts neatly folded. There were also two bottles of shampoo and two bottles of after shave lotion. Muda and the boy were gone, back into the jungle the way they had come. Mohammed had been right. They preferred the jungle to civilization.

This wasn't the last time I saw Muda. I made subsequent journeys into the Malay jungles with game warden Mohammed Kahn, and on several occasions Muda guided us.

He came down river whenever he pleased and departed when the mood suited him. He guided us but he never had the desire to return with us to civilization. Once was enough. I never tired of his company and always looked forward to seeing him when I returned to the forest. And I never tried again to force him to use a modern pack or Western gear.

Two years passed and Mohammed Khan invited me on another expedition. I cabled my reply, and asked if it might be possible that Muda could join us.

When I saw Mohammed at headquarters he gave me the news. Muda was dead.

"How? What happened?" I asked, stunned. "An accident? Tiger? Elephants?"

It was none of these. One day, a few months before, Muda had gone into the jungle, laid down under a tree and died. No one knew the cause of his death, nor had anyone heard him complain of any illness. There was no explanation. To the men of the jungle, there seemed nothing unusual about his passing. It's the way it was, and had to be.

I remember once in the jungle we came upon a group of

Negritoes, perhaps a dozen, and Muda and the others in our party joined them in a long conversation. When it was time to go, Muda simply got up and walked away. There were no farewells or parting words. I didn't think much about it until I learned one of the women was Muda's sister whom he hadn't seen in many years.

"But your sister," I said to Muda, "won't you miss her?"

He couldn't understand why he should be excited about meeting his sister. Then tapping himself on the chest, he said: "I am orang asli. We are all brothers, we are all one."

Perhaps Muda, a jungle man, understood more about the meaning of mankind than our most erudite philosophers. And, for certain, he did know the jungle.

There are other mysterious tribes dwelling in the deep rain forests and hills of Southeast Asia. Iban men of Borneo, once fierce headhunters, let their hair grow long and tie it at the nape of their necks. They are tattooed with ornate designs, from the tips of their chins down to their knees. Both men and women have their ears bored with gaping holes, and some, especially the Kayan women, wear heavy jewelry in their ear lobes that stretches their ears down to their shoulders.

Most Borneo tribes have both respect and fear for the Punans. Some authorities believe Punans are indigenous to the country, the true aborigines. While most other tribes have accepted encroaching civilization, the Punans shun it completely. They are nomadic. They live by gathering fruit and hunting with their primitive weapons.

There are other jungle tribes, and other mystery people of the forests and hills. There might even be people there we don't know about. In Southeast Asia, that's possible.

Chapter 14

A LAST LOOK
Back to Nature

Travel agents have a new market they call "special interest tours," another name for "adventure travel," or, if you wish, "ecotourism." Special interest tours don't come cheap. Even with treks averaging in the hundreds of dollars a day—air fare not included—the adventure market has been moving as fast as rafters shooting down the wild river rapids of New Guinea. The market has nearly doubled every year in the last five making it the fastest growing segment in the travel industry.

Special interest tours are not for everyone, especially for those who like to travel in luxury. Excluding luxury yachts and special cruises, meals on safaris are often prepared by guides who are not graduate chefs from the Escossier School and clients should not expect haute cuisine cooking. And accommodations in the field may be anything from rugged tents to clapboard rest houses without hot water. Even without any water at all. Unlike African safaris, in Asia there are no tented safari camps with heated showers and meals served on white linen table cloths.

One very important fact to keep in mind as you make your plans is that money does not necessarily buy luxury in adventure travel. It buys the most comfortable accommodation available—but comfort in the wilds of Borneo is not the same as comfort in Paris.

Today's adventure travelers are of every age, from their 20s to their 80s, men and women, and they can afford these trips, but their idea of fun is not to play shuffleboard. They grew up in an age of great travel experiences. Rather than take an ocean liner and call it a vacation, as their parents did, they go white water rafting, hot air ballooning and jungle bashing.

Although our roots in adventure travel lie in the early exploits of others, like the mountaineering expeditions of people like Sir Edmund Hillary and Tensing Norkay, and hunting safaris in East Africa made popular by writers Ernest Hemingway and Robert Ruark, we lived them vicariously, through the experience of others. We had to. Not everyone could be a *National Geographic* photographer or a professor with a university grant to go chasing after the rainbow's end. Now with the ease of travel the way it is, and with communications so sophisticated, the ends of the world are at everyone's reach. A business executive can paddle up a wild river in Borneo and be no further away from his office than the lap top computer and portable fax that he carries with him. He can conduct his business from a tent as well as from his Madison Avenue office.

"Safety is a major consideration," one travel agent emphasized. "If you can guarantee a client that it's safe, that he or she won't get hurt, then his business is yours."

In the early days many outings were offered without indication of the physical skills required, and some early adventurers got more than they bargained for.

Virtually every tour operator today grades the physical demands of each trip he has to offer from least to most strenuous. While the rating scales are not uniform from operator to operator, something similar to an "easy," "moderate," "average," "difficult" and "strenuous" ranking can usually be found in brochures and booklets provided by operators.

One last note about special tours: you can never be exactly sure it will turn out the way the brochures say. It's no fault of the operators. You can spend night after night in a tree hide in the Taman Nagara National Park in Malaysia and never see a single tiger or a wild buffalo, but that doesn't mean they are not there.

Likewise, few tours are strapped to rigid itineraries. Instead, while you may know generally where you'll be on a given day, it's no guarantee. That's part of the excitement of adventure travel.

Before you join a special tour, first, find out everything you can about the different companies and tours. Read all brochures and magazines you can get your hands on; talk to people who have taken adventure trips before; talk to the client service people at the companies themselves; and ask the companies for the names and phone numbers of people in the area who have traveled with that company before—they can give you valuable inside perspectives on and information about the company's style and service.

If companies don't want to put you in touch with people who have had taken the tour before, then beware. Find another company.

Another fact you should be aware of is that even after you reserve a place on a tour, the tour company may cancel your trip if it doesn't sign up enough clients. Not all companies operate this way. One exception to the rule is Thai International's Royal Orchid Holidays. Even if there is as little as two people, the tour is still on.

Regardless, you should have an alternative trip in mind just in case your dream trip gets canceled no matter what company or operator it's with.

We are living in a back-to-nature era with environmental concern. Today's tour operations often begin with small groups of adventurers sharing their experiences and expertise with one another. Leading the way are trekkers and bikers, the true forerunners. From this comes interests in river rafting, mountain climbing, scuba diving and jungle safari with cameras, not guns.

Lofty mountains, sunken treasures, lost cities, forbidden shores, dark caves, endless horizons, indeed, an exciting world is out there, awaiting us. All we need do is go and seek it. It's there, believe me.

The author, who has spent most of his life in Asia and the South Pacific, strikes a pose beside a stone Hindu god in Kathmandu. Photo by Robin Dannhorn.

ABOUT THE AUTHOR

An introduction to an author and his work is usually done at the beginning of a book. Most often readers skip the introduction, which I felt might happen here. But I knew by the time readers reached the final chapter, they would wonder who is this writer, Harold Stephens. Does he write fact or fiction. Has he done all those things he talks about? Thus in this case, I felt it appropriate to tell readers about the author.

Many years have passed since I met Harold Stephens, whom everyone calls Steve, but I will remember well that first time. How could I forget? I was then the editor of *Sawasdee,* the in-flight magazine for Thai Airways International, and ensconced in my Hong Kong office, way behind in my work, praying there would be no interruptions, when in came this deeply tanned, well built, incredibly energetic writer with a glint in his eye and a "few ideas for magazine articles."

I made it fairly clear that I had work to do and at first I listened politely and without much interest; but as he spoke of the Asia he knew, I began to become more and more intrigued by his extraordinary tales. As he spoke of crumbling kingdoms, lost cities, buried treasures, head-hunting aborigines, impassable rain forests, I became completely entranced. Into the late afternoon he talked—of a Greek who had risen to great power in Siam, of a Portuguese who had practically ruled Burma, of an Englishman who had carved out his own kingdom in which he was known as the White Rajah. And then he spoke of present-day foreigners living in Asia whom he had come to know and whose stories he had collected—from innkeepers in Nepal to artists in northern Thailand. Late afternoon gave way to evening, and still he filled my office with vivid depictions of all the wonderful, exciting things happening in Asia, many adventures that he experienced aboard his schooner, *Third Sea*, a ship he mastered throughout the seas and rivers of Asia and the South Pacific.

I found it impossible to ask him to leave, and as we continued our conversation from office to a local pub, I began to wonder if this man was the incarnation of the Ancient

Mariner or of a Conradian First Mate on leave from his clipper ship or of an Indonesian puppet master, a *dalang*, whose shadow-plays mesmerize village audiences as they dance across a countryside screen.

Late that evening, by the time Steve and I were three sheets to the wind, I had agreed to publish some of his articles, but I was a bit concerned as to how much of his adventures were real and how much was fantasy. But as the years passed and "Steve" and I became friends, I began to realize he was the real thing. In an age when every other tourist just back from a canned group tour proudly shows off his "Adventurer" T-shirt or "World Traveler" bumper sticker, Harold Stephens turned out to be the genuine article. He had "been there when" and he was still exploring, still learning, still writing.

I have discovered that one of the best traits in Steve's personality is his genuine enthusiasm. He does not have it in him to become jaded or bored—he is too full of zest for life; too full of energy for adventure. Another wonderful trait is his willingness to share what he knows with anyone who asks. That's why he is such a marvelous writer, and for which reason I ended up publishing many dozens of his yarns. Just this year at a book fair in Los Angeles, another author spotted me in a hallway and shook my hand and thanked me profusely for introducing him to Steve. He couldn't believe how helpful and generous Steve was. And I could tell that much of Steve's excitement about travel in Asia had rubbed off on this man as well. In every bookstore in which Steve gives a talk, in every school and university, in every social club, people crowd around to hear of his adventures and the romance of travel. He can grab an audience and hold them, as he did to me the first time we met.

Steve's enthusiasm can be dangerous at times, especially with happy, seeming contented married couples. A married couple, for instance, who invites Harold Stephens to dinner is in for trouble. Because Steve represents freedom and adventure, and after listening to his incredibly romantic tales of Asian intrigue, many people want to chuck what they are doing and join him in his travels. Wives end up shouting at their husbands, "Why don't you go off with Stephens if you think it's so great," and they storm away from the table, banging doors after them. Sometimes it happens the other way. It's the wife who is ready to leave.

I think that Harold Stephens is a worthy representative of those such as W. Somerset Maugham who came before him. Maugham wrote: "It seemed to me that by a long journey to some far distant country I might renew myself . . . I journeyed to the Far East. I went looking for adventure and romance, and so I found them . . . but I found also something I had never expected. I found a new self." And, like Maugham, Steve understands that the ultimate journey is within.

While researching *Hangman's Point*, a novel set in Hong Kong in 1857, I crewed aboard the *HMS Rose*, an replica of a 24-gun English frigate; and there I saw for myself the truth of Steve's belief that the beauty and traditions of Asia are still out there if we are willing to look for them.

The first night I came topside to take my watch, there was little light on deck, and I stepped out into an unfamiliar world of complete darkness. Above was a sky more full of stars than I had ever seen. And in the blackness, I saw the glow of a cigarette; the only sign that, in the midst of this immense, dramatic, almost unimaginable landscape, another human being was somewhere near. I could hear the wind singing in the rigging overhead, the slight complaint of sails as they cracked in the wind, the clattering of the blocks against masts and the sea striking against the bow as we drove into the night — and the worlds of Joseph Conrad and Somerset Maugham and Harold Stephens had come to life.

Dean Barrett. Author
New York City, February 2000
Memoirs of a Bangkok Warrior
Hangman's Point: a Novel of Hong Kong
Kingdom of Make-Believe: a Novel of Thailand

Index